enVision™ Algebra 1

Student Companion

SAVVAS
LEARNING COMPANY

ISBN-13: 978-0-328-9
ISBN-10:   0-328-9

Contents

enVision Algebra 1

About the Authors

Authors

Dan Kennedy, Ph.D

- Classroom teacher and the Lupton Distinguished Professor of Mathematics at the Baylor School in Chattanooga, TN
- Co-author of textbooks *Precalculus: Graphical, Numerical, Algebraic* and *Calculus: Graphical, Numerical, Algebraic, AP Edition*
- Past chair of the College Board's AP Calculus Development Committee.
- Previous Tandy Technology Scholar and Presidential Award winner

Eric Milou, Ed.D

- Professor of Mathematics, Rowan University, Glassboro, NJ
- Member of the author team for Savvas' **enVision**math**2.0** 6-8
- Member of National Council of Teachers of Mathematics (NCTM) feedback/advisory team for the Common Core State Standards
- Author of *Teaching Mathematics to Middle School Students*

Christine D. Thomas, Ph.D

- Professor of Mathematics Education at Georgia State University, Atlanta, GA
- President of the Association of Mathematics Teacher Educators (AMTE)
- Past NCTM Board of Directors Member
- Past member of the editorial panel of the NCTM journal *Mathematics Teacher*
- Past co-chair of the steering committee of t North American chapter of the Internationa Group of the Psychology of Mathematics Education

Rose Mary Zbiek, Ph.D

- Professor of Mathematics Education, Pennsylvania State University, College Park, PA
- Series editor for the NCTM *Essential Understanding* project

Contributing Author

Al Cuoco, Ph.D

- Lead author of CME Project, a National Science Foundation (NSF)-funded high school curriculum
- Team member to revise the Conference Board of the Mathematical Sciences (CBMS) recommendations for teach preparation and professional development
- Co-author of several books published by the Mathematical Association of America and t American Mathematical Society
- Consultant to the writers of the Common Core State Standards for Mathematics and t PARCC Content Frameworks for high school mathematics

CRITIQUE & EXPLAIN

Cindy and Victor are playing a math game. The winner must get three in a row of the same type of real number and justify how the numbers are alike. Cindy said she won because she was able to get three rational numbers on a diagonal. Victor said he won with three positive numbers in a column.

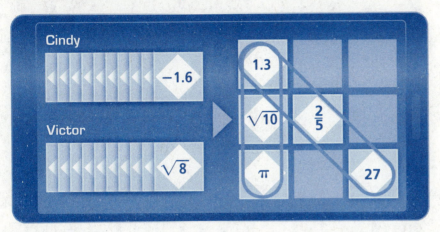

A. Can both players say they won, for different reasons? Explain.

B. Reason Can you make other groups using the numbers shown that are all the same kind of real number? In how many ways can you do this? Ⓒ **MP.2**

HABITS OF MIND

Construct Arguments Cindy says that $\frac{1}{3}$ is an irrational number because the fraction form doesn't terminate. Construct an argument to support or refute Cindy's position. Ⓒ **MP.3**

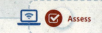 ☑ Assess

EXAMPLE 1 ☑ **Try It!** **Understand Sets and Subsets**

1. Which numbers in set *A* are elements in both the subset of odd numbers and the subset of multiples of 3?

HABITS OF MIND

Generalize Can a number of a set also be an element of more than one subset? Explain. Ⓒ **MP.8**

EXAMPLE 2 ☑ **Try It!** **Compare and Order Real Numbers**

2. Order each set of numbers from least to greatest.

a. $0.25, \sqrt{\frac{1}{9}}, \frac{6}{25}$

b. $\sqrt{\frac{121}{25}}, 2.25, \sqrt{5}$

EXAMPLE 3   ☑ **Try It!** Operations With Rational Numbers

3. Is the quotient of two rational numbers always a rational number? Explain.

EXAMPLE 4   ☑ **Try It!** Operations With Rational and Irrational Numbers

4. Is the difference of a rational number and an irrational number always irrational? Explain.

HABITS OF MIND

Reason When is the square root of a number irrational? Give an example. © **MP.2**

✓ Do You UNDERSTAND?

1. **ESSENTIAL QUESTION** How can you classify the results of operations on real numbers?

2. Communicate Precisely Explain why the sum of a rational number and an irrational number is always irrational. © **MP.6**

3. Vocabulary Are the rational numbers a *subset* of the *set* of all real numbers? Are the rational numbers a *subset* of the irrational numbers? Explain?

4. Error Analysis Jacinta says that the product of a positive and a negative rational number is always irrational. Explain her error. © **MP.3**

5. Reason Let $D = \{-2, -1, 0, 1, 2\}$. Is D a subset of itself? Explain. © **MP.2**

Do You KNOW HOW?

Determine whether set B is a subset of set A.

6. $A = \{0, 1, 2, 3, 4\}$
$B = \{1, 2\}$

7. $A = \{2, 3, 5, 7, 11\}$
$B = \{3, 5, 7, 9, 11\}$

Order each set of numbers from least to greatest.

7. $\sqrt{200}, 14, \frac{41}{3}$

8. $\frac{2}{3}, \sqrt{\frac{9}{16}}, 0.6$

9. The park shown is in the shape of a square. Is its perimeter rational or irrational?

Area = 24,200 yd²

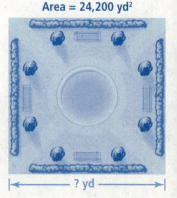

|← ? yd →|

🔵 **MODEL & DISCUSS**

Joshua is going kayaking with a group during one of his vacation days. In his vacation planning, he budgeted $50 for a kayak rental.

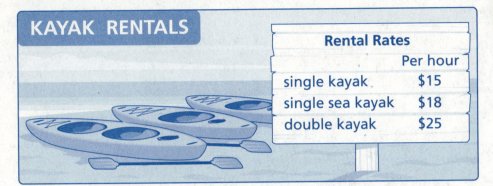

KAYAK RENTALS

Rental Rates	
	Per hour
single kayak	$15
single sea kayak	$18
double kayak	$25

A. How can Joshua determine the number of hours he can rent a kayak for himself? Describe two different options.

B. Joshua found out that there is a $25 nonrefundable equipment fee in addition to the hourly rates. How does this requirement change the mathematics of the situation?

C. **Look for Relationships** How do the processes you used for parts A and B differ? How are they the same? Ⓒ **MP.7**

- - - - - - - - - - - - - - - -
HABITS OF MIND

Make Sense and Persevere How did you determine which operations are needed to solve the problem? Ⓒ **MP.1**

EXAMPLE 1 ☑ **Try It!** **Solve Linear Equations**

1. Solve the equation $4 + \frac{3x-1}{2} = 9$. Explain the reasons why you chose your solution method.

HABITS OF MIND

Communicate Precisely How can you check that the value of the variable makes the equation true? Ⓒ **MP.6**

EXAMPLE 2 ☑ **Try It!** **Solve Consecutive Integer Problems**

2. The sum of three consecutive odd integers is 57. What are the three integers?

EXAMPLE 3 ☑ **Try It!** **Use Linear Equations to Solve Mixture Problems**

3. If the lab technician needs 30 liters of a 25% acid solution, how many liters of the 10% and the 30% acid solutions should she mix to get what she needs?

Assess

EXAMPLE 4 **Try It!** Use Linear Equations to Solve Problems

4. The same four friends buy tickets for two shows on consecutive nights. They use a coupon for $5 off each ticket. They pay a total of $416 for 8 tickets. Write and solve an equation to find the original price of the tickets.

EXAMPLE 5 **Try It!** Solve Work and Time Problems

5. LaTanya leaves her house at 12:30 P.M. and bikes at 12 mi/h to Marta's house. She stays at Marta's house for 90 min. Both girls walk back to LaTanya's house at 2.5 mi/h. They arrive at LaTanya's house at 3:30 P.M. How far is Marta's house from LaTanya's house?

HABITS OF MIND

Look for Relationships What patterns can you identify in the solutions for Examples 3, 4, and 5? © **MP.7**

Do You UNDERSTAND?

1. **? ESSENTIAL QUESTION** How do you create equations and use them to solve problems?

2. **Reason** What is a first step to solving for x in the equation $9x - 7 = 10$? How would you check your solution? Ⓒ **MP.2**

3. **Use Structure** For an equation with fractions, why is it helpful to multiply both sides of the equation by the LCD? Ⓒ **MP.7**

4. **Error Analysis** Venetta knows that 1 mi ≈ 1.6 km. To convert 5 mi/h to km/h, she multiplies 5 mi/h by $\frac{1 \text{ mi}}{1.6 \text{ km}}$. What error does Venetta make? Ⓒ **MP.3**

Do You KNOW HOW?

Solve each equation.

5. $4b + 14 = 22$

6. $-6k - 3 = 39$

7. $15 - 2(3 - 2x) = 46$

8. $\frac{2}{3}y - \frac{2}{5} = 5$

9. **Mathematical Modeling** Terrence walks at a pace of 2 mi/h to the theater and watches a movie for 2 h and 15 min. He rides back home, taking the same route, on the bus that travels at a rate of 40 mi/h. The entire trip takes 3.5 h. How far along this route is Terrence's house from the theater? Explain.

EXPLORE & REASON

Some friends want to see a movie that is showing at two different theaters in town. They plan to share 3 tubs of popcorn during the movie.

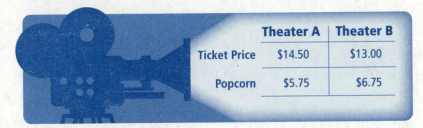

	Theater A	Theater B
Ticket Price	$14.50	$13.00
Popcorn	$5.75	$6.75

A. Construct Arguments Which movie theater should the friends choose? Explain. © MP.3

B. For what situation would the total cost at each theater be exactly the same? Explain.

C. There are different methods to solving this problem. Which do you think is the best? Why?

HABITS OF MIND

Make Sense and Persevere What assumptions did you make that helped you work through the Explore & Reason? © MP.1

EXAMPLE 1 ☑ **Try It!** Solve Equations With a Variable on Both Sides

1. Solve each equation.

    a. $100(z - 0.2) = -10(5z + 0.8)$ b. $\frac{5}{8}(16d + 24) = 6(d - 1) + 1$

EXAMPLE 2 ☑ **Try It!** Understand Equations with Infinitely Many or No Solutions

2. Solve each equation. Is the equation an identity? Explain.

    a. $t - 27 = -(27 - t)$ b. $16(4 - 3m) = 96\left(-\frac{m}{2} + 1\right)$

HABITS OF MIND

Construct Arguments One student maintains that the order in which terms are collected on each side of an equation does not matter. Construct an argument to support or refute the student's position. ⓒ **MP.3**

EXAMPLE 3   ☑ **Try It!** **Solve Mixture Problems**

3. How many pounds of Arabica coffee should you mix with 5 pounds of Robusta coffee to make a coffee blend that costs $12.00 per pound?

HABITS OF MIND

Generalize How can you determine whether an equation has infinitely many or no solutions? Ⓒ **MP.8**

EXAMPLE 4   ☑ **Try It!** **Use Equations to Solve Problems**

4. Cameron's friend tells him of another service that has a $15 joining fee but charges $0.80 per song. At what number of songs does this new service become a less expensive option to Cameron's current service?

Do You UNDERSTAND?

1. **ESSENTIAL QUESTION** How do you create equations with a variable on both sides and use them to solve problems?

2. **Vocabulary** Why does it make sense to describe an equation that has infinitely many solutions as an *identity*?

3. **Error Analysis** Isabel says that the equation $x - 2 = -(x - 2)$ has no solution because a number can never be equal to its opposite. Explain the error Isabel made. **© MP.3**

4. **Look for Relationships** You are solving an equation with a variable on each side. Does the side on which you choose to isolate the variable affect the solution? Why might you choose one side over the other? **© MP.7**

Do You KNOW HOW?

Solve each equation.

5. $5(2x + 6) = 8x + 48$

6. $-3(8 + 3h) = 5h + 4$

7. $2(y - 6) = 3(y - 4) - y$

8. $8x - 4 = 2(4x - 4)$

9. For how many games is the total cost of bowling equal for the two bowling establishments?

Family Bowling		
Cost (dollars)	Game	4.00
	Shoes	1.00
Knight Owl Bowling		
Cost (dollars)	Game	3.75
	Shoes	2.00

STRIKE!
Bowling & Entertaiment

12 **TOPIC 1** Solving Equations and Inequalities

Go Online | SavvasRealize.com

MODEL & DISCUSS

Nora drew a nonsquare rectangle. Then she drew the length of each side from end to end to make a line segment to represent the perimeter.

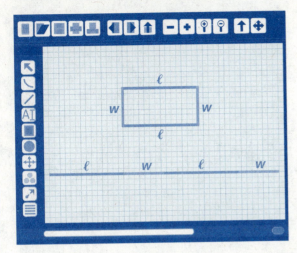

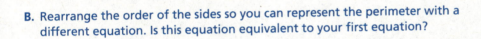

A. Write an equation that represents the perimeter of the model shown.

B. Rearrange the order of the sides so you can represent the perimeter with a different equation. Is this equation equivalent to your first equation?

C. Use Structure How many different ways can you express the relationship in parts A and B? Are any of them more useful than others? © MP.7

HABITS OF MIND

Construct Arguments What mathematical argument supports your response in part C? © MP.3

EXAMPLE 1 ☑ **Try It!** Rewrite Literal Equations

1. What equation can Janet use to calculate the principal amount?

EXAMPLE 2 ☑ **Try It!** Use Literal Equations to Solve Problems

2. Sarah is going to the store 2.5 miles away. She has only 15 min to get there before they close. At what average speed must she ride to get to the store before they close?

HABITS OF MIND

Use Structure How is solving equations with numbers the same as solving equations with only variables? © MP.7

EXAMPLE 3  **Try It!** Rewrite a Formula

3. Write the formula for the area of a triangle, $A = \frac{1}{2}bh$ in terms of h. Find the height of a triangle when $A = 18$ in.^{2} and $b = 9$ in.

EXAMPLE 4  **Try It!** Apply Formulas

4. The high temperature on a given winter day is 5°F. What is the temperature in °C?

HABITS OF MIND

Reason How are the variables in the temperature conversion formula related? **© MP.2**

☑ Do You UNDERSTAND?

1. ❓ **ESSENTIAL QUESTION** How is rewriting literal equations useful when solving problems?

2. **Communicate Precisely** How is solving $2x + c = d$ similar to solving $2x + 1 = 9$ for x? How are they different? How can you use $2x + c = d$ to solve $2x + 1 = 9$? Ⓒ **MP.6**

3. **Vocabulary** Explain how literal equations and formulas are related.

4. **Error Analysis** Dyani began solving the equation $g = \frac{x-1}{k}$ for x by using the Addition Property of Equality. Explain Dyani's error. Then describe how to solve for x. Ⓒ **MP.3**

Do You KNOW HOW?

Solve each literal equation for the given variable.

5. $y = x + 12$; x

6. $n = \frac{4}{5}(m + 7)$; m

7. Use your equation from Exercise 6 to find m when $n = 40$.

8. William got scores of q_1, q_2, and q_3 on three quizzes.

   a. Write a formula for the average x of all three quizzes.

   b. William got an 85 and an 88 on the first two quizzes. What formula can William use to determine the score he needs on the third quiz to get an average of 90? What score does he need?

MODEL & DISCUSS

Skyler competes in the high jump event at her school. She hopes to tie or break some records at the next meet.

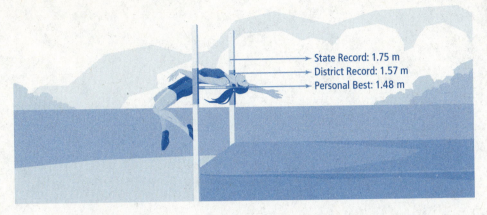

State Record: 1.75 m
District Record: 1.57 m
Personal Best: 1.48 m

A. Write and solve an equation to find *x*, the number of meters Skyler must add to her personal best to tie the district record.

B. Look for Relationships Rewrite your equation as an inequality to represent the situation where Skyler *breaks* the district record. How is the value of *x* in the inequality related to the value of *x* in the equation? © MP.7

C. How many meters does Skyler need to add to her personal best to break the state record?

HABITS OF MIND

Make Sense and Persevere What strategy did you use to answer the questions? What other strategy might you have used? © MP.1

EXAMPLE 1   ☑ **Try It!** Solve Inequalities

1. Solve each inequality and graph the solution.

    a. $-3(2x + 2) < 10$ **b.** $2(4 - 2x) > 1$

EXAMPLE 2   ☑ **Try It!** Solve an Inequality With Variables on Both Sides

2. Solve $2x - 5 < 5x - 22$. Then graph the solution.

EXAMPLE 3 ☑ **Try It!** **Understand Inequalities With Infinitely Many or No Solutions**

3. Solve each inequality.

a. $-2(4x - 2) < -8x + 4$

b. $-6x - 5 < -3(2x + 1)$

EXAMPLE 4 ☑ **Try It!** **Use Inequalities to Solve Problems**

4. If Florist B increases the cost per rose to $5.20, for what number of roses is it less expensive to order from Florist A? From Florist B?

HABITS OF MIND

Look for Structure How is solving an inequality with variables on one side similar to and different from solving an inequality with variables on both sides? ⓒ **MP.7**

Do You UNDERSTAND?

1. **ESSENTIAL QUESTION** How are the solutions of an inequality different from the solution of an equation?

2. **Reason** How is dividing each side of $x > 0$ by a negative value different from dividing each side by a positive value? © **MP.2**

3. **Vocabulary** Give an example of two inequalities that are *equivalent inequalities*. Explain your reasoning.

4. **Error Analysis** Rachel multiplied each side of $x \geq 2$ by 3. She wrote the result as $3x \leq 6$. Explain the error Rachel made. © **MP.3**

Do You KNOW HOW?

Solve each inequality and graph the solution.

5. $\frac{1}{2}x < 6$

6. $-4x \geq 20$

7. $8 \leq -4(x - 1)$

8. $3x - 2 > 4 - 3x$

9. Lourdes plans to jog at least 1.5 miles. Write and solve an inequality to find x, the number of hours that Lourdes will have to jog.

3.75 MPH

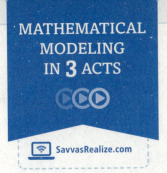

Collecting Cans

Many schools and community centers organize canned food drives and donate the food collected to area food pantries or homeless shelters.

A teacher may hold a contest for the student who collects the most cans. The teacher will track the number of cans each student brings in. Sometimes students have their own ways of keeping track. You'll see how some students kept track in the Mathematical Modeling in 3 Acts lesson.

ACT 1

1. What is the first question that comes to mind after watching the video?

2. Write down the Main Question you will answer.

3. Make an initial conjecture that answers this Main Question.

4. Explain how you arrived at your conjecture.

5. Write a number that you know is too small.

6. Write a number that you know is too large.

ACT 2

7. Use the math that you have learned in the topic to refine your conjecture.

ACT 3

8. Is your refined conjecture between the highs and lows you set up earlier?

9. Did your refined conjecture match the actual answer exactly? If not, what might explain the difference?

1-6
Compound Inequalities

SavvasRealize.com

EXPLORE & REASON

Hana has some blue paint. She wants to lighten the shade, so she mixes in 1 cup of white paint. The color is still too dark, so Hana keeps mixing in 1 cup of white paint at a time. After adding 4 cups, she decides the color is too light.

plus 4 c white paint

plus 1 c white paint

A. Explain in words how much paint Hana should have added initially to get the shade she wants.

B. Model With Mathematics Represent your answer to part A with one or more inequalities. MP.4

C. Hana decides that she likes the shades of blue that appear in between adding 1 cup and 4 cups of white paint. How can you represent the number of cups of white paint that yield the shades Hana prefers?

HABITS OF MIND

Mathematical Modeling If the solution to an inequality includes all the values that are in between two values, how can you show that on a number line? MP.4

EXAMPLE 1    **Try It! Understand Compound Inequalities**

1. Write a compound inequality for the graph.

$$\xleftarrow{\qquad\overset{\oplus}{\underset{-2}{\quad}}\; \underset{0}{|}\qquad\qquad \underset{6}{\bullet}\qquad}\rightarrow$$

EXAMPLE 2    **Try It! Solve a Compound Inequality Involving *Or***

2. Solve the compound inequality $-3x + 2 > -7$ or $2(x - 2) \geq 6$. Graph the solution.

HABITS OF MIND

Make Sense of Problems How does representing a compound inequality solution on a graph help show the solution accurately? © **MP.1**

EXAMPLE 3 ☑ **Try It!** Solve a Compound Inequality Involving *And*

3. Solve the compound inequality $-2(x + 1) < 4$ and $4x + 1 \leq -3$. Graph the solution.

EXAMPLE 4 ☑ **Try It!** Solve Problems Involving Compound Inequalities

4. Suppose River has new treats that are 10 calories each. How many of the new treats can she have and remain in her calorie range?

HABITS OF MIND

Communicate Precisely Describe the solution of an inequality involving *or* and an inequality involving *and*. Ⓒ **MP.6**

Do You UNDERSTAND?

1. **ESSENTIAL QUESTION** What are compound inequalities and how are their solutions represented?

2. **Look for Relationships** When $a < b$, how is the graph of $x > a$ and $x < b$ similar to the graph of $x > a$? How is it different? Ⓒ **MP.7**

3. **Vocabulary** A *compound* is defined as a *mixture*. Make a conjecture as to why the term *compound inequality* includes the word *compound*.

4. **Error Analysis** Kona graphed the compound inequality $x > 2$ or $x > 3$ by graphing $x > 3$. Explain Kona's error. Ⓒ **MP.3**

Do You KNOW HOW?

Write a compound inequality for each graph.

5.
    −4 −1 0

6. ![number line]
    0   2   8

Solve each compound inequality and graph the solution.

7. $4x - 1 > 3$ and $-2(3x - 4) \geq -16$

8. $2(4x + 3) \geq -10$ or $-5x - 15 > 5$

9. Nadeem plans to ride her bike between 12 mi and at most 15 mi. Write and solve an inequality to model how many hours Nadeem will be riding.

MODEL & DISCUSS

Amelia is participating in a 60-mile spin-a-thon. Her spin bike keeps track of the simulated number of miles she travels. She plans to take a 15-minute break within 5 miles of riding 30 miles.

Amelia spins at a constant 22 mph.

Spin-a-thon Schedule	
Event	**Time**
Start spinning	10:00 A.M.
Stop for break	■
Resume spinning	■

A. Write a compound inequality that models the number of miles Amelia spins before taking a break.

B. How is the number of miles Amelia spins before she takes a break related to the amount of time before she takes a break?

C. Make Sense and Persevere About how many hours will Amelia spin before she takes a break? Discuss how you could use your mathematical model to complete the spin-a-thon schedule. Ⓒ **MP.1**

HABITS OF MIND

Reason How is the time Amelia is spinning related to the distance she spins? Ⓒ **MP.2**

EXAMPLE 1 ☑ **Try It!** Understand Absolute Value Equations

1. Solve.

a. $6 = |x| - 2$ b. $2|x + 5| = 4$ c. $|3x - 6| = 12$

EXAMPLE 2 ☑ **Try It!** Apply an Absolute Value Equation

2. What will be the minimum and maximum time that Kennedy will travel if she resets her cruising speed to 20 mi/h?

HABITS OF MIND

Generalize How is solving an absolute value equation similar to solving a regular equation? How is it different? © **MP.8**

EXAMPLE 3   ☑ **Try It!** **Understand Absolute Value Inequalities**

3. Solve and graph the solutions of each inequality.

  a. $|x| > 15$ **b.** $|x| \leq 7$

EXAMPLE 4   ☑ **Try It!** **Write an Absolute Value Inequality**

4. If the debate team increased their limit to $200 plus or minus $20, would they be able to afford Hotel D at $55 per night? Explain.

HABITS OF MIND

Look for Relationships What do you notice about absolute value inequalities that is similar to compound inequalities? Ⓒ **MP.7**

Do You UNDERSTAND?

1. **ESSENTIAL QUESTION** Why does the solution for an absolute value equation or inequality typically result in a pair of equations or inequalities?

2. **Reason** How is solving an absolute value equation similar to solving an equation that does not involve absolute value? How is it different? © MP.2

3. **Vocabulary** Describe how you would explain to another student why the *absolute value* of a number cannot be negative.

4. **Error Analysis** Yumiko solved $|x| > 5$ by solving $x > -5$ and $x < 5$. Explain the error Yumiko made. © MP.3

Do You KNOW HOW?

Solve each absolute value equation.

5. $5 = |x| + 3$

6. $|2x - 8| = 16$

Solve each absolute value inequality. Graph the solution.

7. $|3x - 6| \geq 9$

8. $|4x - 12| \leq 20$

9. On a road trip, Andrew plans to use his cruise control for 125 mi, plus or minus 20 mi. Write and solve an equation to find the minimum and maximum number of hours for Andrew's road trip.

MODEL & DISCUSS

Alani wants to buy a $360 bicycle. She is considering two payment options. The image shows Option A, which consists of making an initial down payment then smaller, equal-sized weekly payments. Option B consists of making 6 equal payments over 6 weeks.

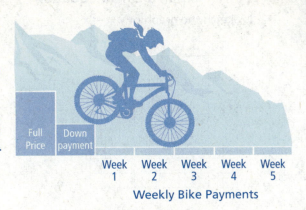

Weekly Bike Payments

A. What factors should Alani take into consideration before deciding between Option A and Option B?

B. Communicate Precisely Suppose Alani could modify Option A and still pay off the bike in 5 weeks. Describe the relationship between the down payment and the weekly payments. Ⓒ **MP.6**

HABITS OF MIND

Look for Relationships What do you notice about the relationship among the amount of the payment, the number of payments, and the time it takes to pay off the loan? Ⓒ **MP.7**

EXAMPLE 1   **Try It!** **Graph a Linear Equation**

1. Sketch the graph of $y = -\frac{3}{4}x - 5$.

HABITS OF MIND

Reason What do the numbers represent in a linear equation in slope-intercept form? Ⓒ **MP.2**

EXAMPLE 2   **Try It!** **Write an Equation from a Graph**

2. Write the equation of the line in slope-intercept form.

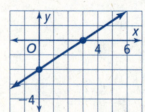

EXAMPLE 3   ☑ **Try It!** **Understand Slope-Intercept Form**

3. Write the equation in slope-intercept form of the line that passes through the points (5, 4) and (−1, 6).

EXAMPLE 4   ☑ **Try It!** **Interpret Slope and *y*-Intercept**

4. Use information from Example 4 to write the equation in slope-intercept form. Find the *x*-intercept of the graph of the equation. What does the *x*-intercept mean in terms of the situation?

HABITS OF MIND

Construct Arguments How does the slope of a line given in slope-intercept form with a fractional coefficient of *x* compare to the slope of a line with a whole number coefficient of *x*? Ⓒ **MP.3**

Do You UNDERSTAND?

1. ? ESSENTIAL QUESTION What information does the slope-intercept form of a linear equation reveal about a line?

2. Communicate Precisely How are the graphs of $y = 2x + 1$ and $y = -2x + 1$ similar? How are they different? © **MP.6**

3. Error Analysis To graph $y = \frac{2}{3}x + 4$, Emaan plots one point at (0, 4) and a second point 2 units right and 3 units up at (2, 7). He then draws a line through (0, 4) and (2, 7). What error did Emaan make? © **MP.3**

4. Make Sense and Persevere When writing the equation of a line in slope-intercept form, how can you determine the value of m in $y = mx + b$ if you know the coordinates of two points on the line? © **MP.1**

Do You KNOW HOW?

Sketch the graph of each equation.

5. $y = 2x - 5$

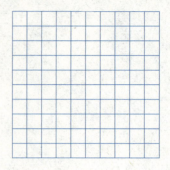

6. $y = -\frac{3}{4}x + 2$

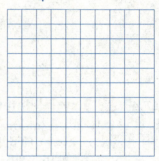

Identify the slope and y-intercept of the line for each equation.

7. $y = -5x - \frac{3}{4}$ **8.** $y = \frac{1}{4}x + 5$

Write the equation of each line in slope-intercept form.

9. 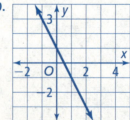   **10.**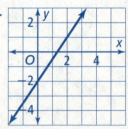

11. A line that passes through (3, 1) and (0, −3)

12. A line that passes through (−1, −5) and (2, 4)

CRITIQUE & EXPLAIN

Paul and Seth know that one point on a line is (4, 2) and the slope of the line is −5. Each student derived an equation relating x and y.

SavvasRealize.com

Paul	Seth
$y = mx + b$	$m = \dfrac{y_2 - y_1}{x_2 - x_1}$
$2 = -5(4) + b$	
$2 = -20 + b$	$-5 = \dfrac{y - 2}{x - 4}$
$22 = b$	
$y = -5x + 22$	$-5(x - 4) = y - 2$

A. Do the two equations represent the same line? Construct a mathematical argument to support your answer.

B. Make Sense and Persevere Generate a table of values for each equation. How can you reconcile the tables with the equations? Ⓒ **MP.1**

HABITS OF MIND

Model With Mathematics How could you represent the equations to show they are equivalent? Explain. Ⓒ **MP.4**

EXAMPLE 1 ☑ **Try It!** **Understand Point–Slope Form of a Linear Equation**

1. Describe the steps needed to find the *y*-intercept of the graph using point-slope form.

EXAMPLE 2 ☑ **Try It!** **Write an Equation in Point–Slope Form**

2. Write an equation of the line that passes through (2, −1) and (−3, 3).

HABITS OF MIND

Generalize Explain why the equation of a vertical line cannot be written in point–slope form. Ⓒ **MP.8**

EXAMPLE 3 ☑ **Try It! Sketch the Graph of a Linear Equation in Point-Slope Form**

3. Sketch the graph of $y + 2 = \frac{1}{2}(x - 3)$.

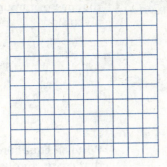

EXAMPLE 4 ☑ **Try It! Apply Linear Equations**

4. Rewrite the point-slope form equation from Example 4 in slope-intercept form. What does the *y*-intercept represent in terms of the situation?

HABITS OF MIND

Make Sense and Persevere When is it appropriate to write the equation of a line in point-slope form rather than in slope-intercept form? Ⓒ **MP.1**

✓ Do You UNDERSTAND?

1. ❓ **ESSENTIAL QUESTION** What information does the point-slope form of a linear equation reveal about a line?

2. Use Structure If you know a point on a line and the slope of the line, how can you find another point on the line? Ⓒ **MP.7**

3. Error Analysis Denzel identified (3, 2) as a point on the line $y - 2 = \frac{2}{3}(x + 3)$. What is the error that Denzel made? Ⓒ **MP.3**

4. Generalize You know the slope and one point on a line that is not the y-intercept. Why might you write the equation in point-slope form instead of slope-intercept form? Ⓒ **MP.8**

Do You KNOW HOW?

Write the equation of the line in point-slope form that passes through the given point with the given slope.

5. (1, 5); $m = -3$ **6.** (−4, 3); $m = 2$

Write an equation of the line in point-slope form that passes through the given points.

7. (4, 2) and (1, 6)

8. (−2, 8) and (7, −4)

9. Write the equation $y - 6 = -5(x + 1)$ in slope-intercept form.

10. Write the equation of the line in point-slope form.

a.
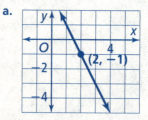

b.
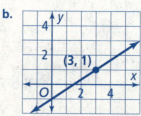

EXPLORE & REASON

Jae makes a playlist of 24 songs for a party. Since he prefers country and rock music, he builds the playlist from those two types of songs.

A. Determine two different combinations of country and rock songs that Jae could use for his playlist.

B. Plot those combinations on graph paper. Extend a line through the points.

C. Model With Mathematics Can you use the line to find other meaningful points? Explain. Ⓒ **MP.4**

- -

HABITS OF MIND

Use Appropriate Tools Why is it helpful to use a graph rather than a table to answer the question? Are there any disadvantages to using a graph? Ⓒ **MP.5**

EXAMPLE 1  **Try It!** **Understand Standard Form of a Linear Equation**

1. Is it easier to find the *x*-intercept of the graph of the equations in Part B using slope-intercept or standard form? Explain.

EXAMPLE 2 **Try It!** **Sketch the Graph of a Linear Equation in Standard Form**

2. Sketch the graph of $4x + 5y = 10$.

EXAMPLE 3 **Try It!** **Relate Standard Form to Horizontal and Vertical Lines**

3. Sketch the graph of each equation.

   a. $3y = -18$ b. $4x = 12$

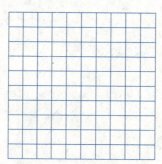   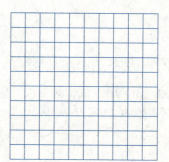

HABITS OF MIND

Generalize Given a linear equation in standard form, can you always find the *x*- and *y*-intercepts? Explain. Ⓒ **MP.8**

EXAMPLE 4 ☑ **Try It!** **Use the Standard Form of a Linear Equation**

4. How does the equation change if Tamira has $60 to spend on a mixture of almonds and cashews? How many pounds of nuts can she buy if she buys only cashews? Only almonds? A mixture of both?

HABITS OF MIND

Model With Mathematics How can you tell when every point on the graph is a solution to the problem? ⒸMP.4

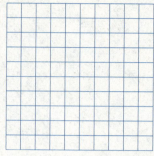
Do You UNDERSTAND?

1. **ESSENTIAL QUESTION** What information does the standard form of a linear equation reveal about a line?

2. **Communicate Precisely** How is the standard form of a linear equation similar to and different from the slope-intercept form? © **MP.6**

3. **Error Analysis** Malcolm says that $y = -1.5x + 4$ in standard form is $1.5x + y = 4$. What is the error that Malcolm made? © **MP.3**

4. **Use Structure** Describe a situation in which the standard form of a linear equation is a more useful than the slope-intercept form. © **MP.7**

Do You KNOW HOW?

Use the *x*- and *y*-intercepts to sketch a graph of each equation.

5. $x + 4y = 8$

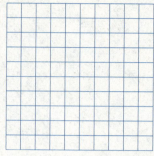

6. $3x - 4y = 24$

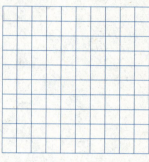

7. $5x = 20$

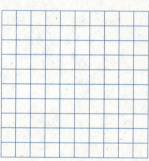

8. $-3y = 9$

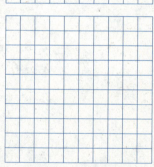

9. Deondra has $12 to spend on a mixture of green and red grapes. What equation can she use to graph a line showing the different amounts of green and red grapes she can buy for $12?

GRAPE SALE!

GREEN
$3/lb

RED
$2/lb

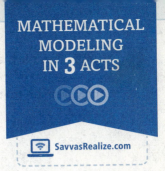

▶ How Tall Is Tall?

The world's tallest person in recorded history was Robert Wadlow. He was 8 feet 11.1 inches tall! Only 5% of the world population is 6 feet 3 inches or taller. What percent of the population would you guess is 7 feet or taller?

We usually use standard units, such as feet and inches or centimeters, to measure length or height. Did you ever wonder why? In the Mathematical Modeling in 3 Acts lesson you'll consider some interesting alternatives.

ACT 1 Identify the Problem

1. What is the first question that comes to mind after watching the video?

How tall is Jay

2. Write down the main question you will answer about what you saw in the video.

How many cups tall is Jay

3. Make an initial conjecture that answers this main question.

76 cups

4. Explain how you arrived at your conjecture.

5. Write a number that you know is too small.

12 cups

6. Write a number that you know is too large.

200 cups

7. What information will be useful to know to answer the main question? How can you get it? How will you use that information?

The height of the cup and lip and Jays height

ACT 2 · Develop a Model

8. Use the math that you have learned in this Topic to refine your conjecture.

lip = 0.6 inches   y = 80

Jay = 80 inches   m = 0.6

cup + lip = 4.6 in.

cup = 4

$80 = 3/5 x + 4.6$
$-4.6 \quad -4.6$

$75.4 = 3/5 x$

$/ \frac{3}{5} \quad / \frac{3}{5}$

$\frac{75.4}{1} \cdot \frac{5}{3}$

$2.\frac{75.4}{5}$

$\overline{3770}$

125

$3\overline{)377}$

$\frac{12}{3}$

ACT 3 · Interpret the Results

9. Is your refined conjecture between the highs and lows you set up earlier?

Yes

10. Did your refined conjecture match the actual answer exactly? If not, what might explain the difference?

No. The height of each cup isn't equal because of the weight of the cups, and the heels of the shoes

EXPLORE & REASON

Graph these three equations using a graphing calculator.

Plot1 Plot2 Plot3
\Y₁ ▩3X+1
\Y₂ ▩3X+2
\Y₃ ▩3X+4
\Y₄=
\Y₅=
\Y₆=
\Y₇=

A. Look for Relationships Choose any two of the lines you graphed. How are they related to each other? © **MP.7**

B. Does your answer to Part A hold for any two lines? Explain.

C. Write another set of three or more equations that have the same relationships as the first three equations.

HABITS OF MIND

Look for Relationships What concepts have you learned previously that were useful in analyzing this problem? © **MP.7**

EXAMPLE 1 **Try It!** Write an Equation of a Parallel Line Parallel to a Given Line

1. Write the equation of the line in slope-intercept form that passes through the point $(-3, 5)$ and is parallel to $y = -\frac{2}{3}x$.

EXAMPLE 2 **Try It!** Understand the Slopes of Perpendicular Lines

2. Why does it make sense that the slopes of perpendicular lines have opposite signs?

EXAMPLE 3 **Try It!** Write an Equation of a Line Perpendicular to a Given Line

3. Write the equation of the line that passes through the point $(4, 5)$ and is perpendicular to the graph of $y = 2x - 3$.

HABITS OF MIND

Communicate Precisely Why do you have to use the term "nonvertical" when working with parallel and perpendicular lines? © **MP.6**

EXAMPLE 4 ☑ **Try It!** **Classify Lines**

4. Are the graphs of the equations *parallel, perpendicular,* or *neither?*

  a. $y = 2x + 6$ and $y = \frac{1}{2}x + 3$

  b. $y = -5x$ and $25x + 5y = 1$

EXAMPLE 5 ☑ **Try It!** **Solve a Real-World Problem**

5. The equation $y = 2x + 7$ represents the North Path on a map.

  a. Find the equation for a path that passes through the point (6, 3) and is parallel to the North Path.

  b. Find the equation for a path that passes through the same point but is perpendicular to North Path.

- -

HABITS OF MIND

Use Structure Explain the advantages of using the slope–intercept form of an equation when determining if two lines are perpendicular or parallel to each other. Ⓒ MP.7

Do You UNDERSTAND?

1. **ESSENTIAL QUESTION** How can the equations of lines help you identify whether the lines are *parallel*, *perpendicular*, or *neither*?

2. **Error Analysis** Dwayne stated that the slope of the line perpendicular to $y = -2x$ is 2. Describe Dwayne's error. Ⓒ **MP.3**

3. **Vocabulary** Describe the difference between the slopes of two parallel lines and the slopes of two perpendicular lines.

4. **Use Structure** Is there one line that passes through the point (3, 5) that is parallel to the lines represented by $y = 2x - 4$ and $y = x - 4$? Explain. Ⓒ **MP.7**

Do You KNOW HOW?

The equation $y = -\frac{3}{4}x + 1$ represents a given a line.

5. Write the equation for the line that passes through (−4, 9) and is parallel to the given line.

6. Write the equation for the line that passes through (6, 6) and is perpendicular to the given line.

Are the graphs of the equations parallel, perpendicular, or neither?

7. $x - 3y = 6$ and $x - 3y = 9$

8. $y = 4x + 1$ and $y = -4x - 2$

9. What equation represents the road that that passes through the point shown and is perpendicular to the road represented by the red line?

EXPLORE & REASON

The desks in a study hall are arranged in rows like the horizontal ones in the picture.

A. What is a reasonable number of rows for the study hall? What is a reasonable number of desks?

B. Look for Structure What number of rows would be impossible? What number of desks would be impossible? Explain. ©️ **MP.7**

C. What do your answers to Parts A and B reveal about what the graph of rows to desks looks like?

HABITS OF MIND

Model with Mathematics What other representations could you use to display the student information? Select and describe one representation. Explain how the information would be presented. ©️ **MP.4**

EXAMPLE 1 ☑ **Try It!** **Recognize Domain and Range**

1. Identify the domain and the range of each function.

a.

x	2	3	4	5	6
y	0	1	2	3	4

b.

x	−3	−1	1	3	4
y	1	3	−2	2	6

EXAMPLE 2 ☑ **Try It!** **Analyze Reasonable Domains and Ranges**

2. Analyze each situation. Identify a reasonable domain and range for each situation. Explain.

a. A bowler pays $2.75 per game.

b. A car travels 25 miles using 1 gallon of gas.

HABITS OF MIND

Make Sense and Persevere How do characteristics of a situation impact the domain of a function that describes it? © MP.1

EXAMPLE 3 ✓ **Try It! Classify Relations and Functions**

3. Is each relation a function? If so, is it one-to-one or not one-to-one??

a.

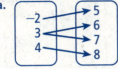

b.

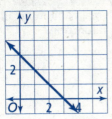

EXAMPLE 4 ✓ **Try It! Identify Constraints on the Domain**

4. Margaret has a monthly clothes budget of $50. She maps the amount of money she spends each month to the number of items of clothing she buys. What constraints are there on the domain?

HABITS OF MIND

Use Appropriate Tools What are the advantages of using mapping diagrams when analyzing functions? Explain. ⓒ **MP.5**

Do You UNDERSTAND?

1. **ESSENTIAL QUESTION** What is a function? Why is domain and range important when defining a function?

2. Vocabulary Maya is tracking the amount of rainfall during a storm. Describe the *domain* and *range* for this situation. Include *continuous* or *discrete* in your description.

3. Reason What can you conclude about the domain and the range of a function if a vertical line at $x = 5$ passes through 2 points? 1 point? No points? Explain. © **MP.2**

4. Error Analysis Felipe states that every relation is a function, but not every function is a relation. Explain Felipe's error. © **MP.3**

Do You KNOW HOW?

5. Use the graph to determine the domain and range of this relation. Is the relation a function?

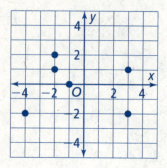

6. For the set of ordered pairs shown, identify the domain and range. Does the relation represent a function?
{(1, 8), (5, 3), (7, 6), (2, 2), (8, 4), (3, 9), (5, 7)}

7. Each day Jacob records the number of laps and the distance he walks, in miles, on a track. Graph the relation and determine whether the distance that Jacob walks is a function of the number of laps.
{(3, 0.75), (6, 1.5), (9, 2.25), (2, 0.5), (7, 1.75), (10, 2.5), (4, 1)}

MODEL & DISCUSS

The flowchart shows the steps of a math puzzle.

A. Try the puzzle with 6 different integers.

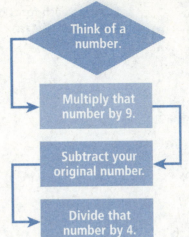

Think of a number.

Multiply that number by 9.

Subtract your original number.

Divide that number by 4.

B. Record each number you try and the result.

C. Make a prediction about what the final number will be for any number. Explain.

D. Use Structure Would your prediction be true for all numbers? Explain. MP.7

HABITS OF MIND
Construct Arguments Is it possible to find a counterexample? © MP.3

EXAMPLE 1 **Try It!** **Evaluate Functions in Function Notation**

1. Evaluate each function for $x = 4$.

  a. $g(x) = -2x - 3$

  $g(4) = -2(4) - 3$

  $g(4) = -8 - 3 = -11$

  b. $h(x) = 7x + 15$

  $h(4) = 7(4) + 15$

  $h(4) = 28 + 15 = 43$

EXAMPLE 2 **Try It!** **Write a Linear Function Rule**

2. Write a linear function for the data in each table using function notation.

a.

x	1	2	3	4
y	6.5	13	19.5	26

b.

x	1	2	3	4
y	1	4	7	10

HABITS OF MIND

Look for Relationships What can the relationship between the values of x and the values of y reveal about a function? © **MP.7**

EXAMPLE 3 ☑ **Try It!** Analyze a Linear Function

3. Sketch the graph of each function.

    a. $f(x) = -x + 1$ b. $f(x) = 3x + 1$

EXAMPLE 4 ☑ **Try It!** Use Linear Functions to Solve Problems

4. In Example 4, how would the function, graph, and equation change if the speed is 4 mph? What is the effect on the domain?

HABITS OF MIND

Reason How is a linear function related to a linear equation? Explain. © **MP.2**

Do You UNDERSTAND?

1. **ESSENTIAL QUESTION** How can you identify a linear function?

2. **Communicate Precisely** Give a real-world example of a function that is linear and one that is not linear. Explain. © **MP.6**

3. **Vocabulary** What is the difference between a *linear function* and a linear equation?

4. **Error Analysis** The cost of using a game facility is $1 for every 12 minutes. Talisa writes the function for the cost per hour as $f(x) = 12x$. Explain Talisa's error. © **MP.3**

Do You KNOW HOW?

Evaluate each function for $x = 2$ and $x = 6$.

5. $f(x) = 4x - 3$

6. $f(x) = -(x - 2)$

7. Sketch the graph of $f(x) = \frac{1}{2}x + 5$.

8. What function models the height of the periscope lens at time t? If the periscope reaches its maximum height after ascending for 22 seconds, what is the maximum height in feet?

24 inches above the surface

ascends at 6 inches per second

Go Online | SavvasRealize.com

CRITIQUE & EXPLAIN

Avery states that the graph of *g* is the same as the graph of *f* with every point shifted vertically. Cindy states that the graph of *g* is the same as the graph of *f* with every point shifted horizontally.

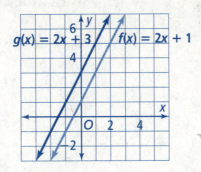

$g(x) = 2x + 3$ $f(x) = 2x + 1$

A. Give an argument to support Avery's statement.

B. Give an argument to support Cindy's statement.

C. **Look for Relationships** What do you know about linear equations that might support either of their statements? Ⓒ **MP.7**

- -

HABITS OF MIND

Generalize Would the same arguments apply to the equations of other pairs of parallel lines? Ⓒ **MP.8**

EXAMPLE 1 ☑ **Try It!** **Vertical Translations of Linear Functions**

1. Let $f(x) = -4x$.

   a. How does the graph of $g(x) = -4x - 3$ compare with the graph of f?

   b. How does the graph of $g(x) = -4x + 1.5$ compare with the graph of f?

EXAMPLE 2 ☑ **Try It!** **Horizontal Translations of Linear Functions**

2. Let $f(x) = 3x + 7$.

   a. How does the graph of $g(x) = 3(x - 4) + 7$ compare with the graph of f?

   b. How does the graph of $g(x) = 3(x + 9.5) + 7$ compare with the graph of f?

HABITS OF MIND

Use Appropriate Tools How does looking at a table of values help you understand translations? ⒸMP.5

☑ Try It! Stretches and Compressions of Linear Functions

3. Let $f(x) = x - 2$.

   a. How does the graph of $g(x) = 0.25(x - 2)$ compare with the graph of f?

   b. How does the graph of $g(x) = 0.5x - 2$ compare with the graph of f?

HABITS OF MIND

Reason How does the relationship between the elements of the domain and the elements of the range relate to transformations of the function? Explain. ⒸMP.2

Do You UNDERSTAND?

1. **ESSENTIAL QUESTION** How does modifying the input or the output of a linear function rule transform its graph?

2. **Vocabulary** Why is the addition or subtraction of *k* to the output of a function considered a *translation*?

3. **Error Analysis** The addition or subtraction of a number to a linear a function always moves the line up or down. Describe the error with this reasoning. Ⓒ **MP.3**

4. **Use Structure** Why does multiplying the input of a linear function change only the slope while multiplying the output changes both the slope and the *y*-intercept? Ⓒ **MP.7**

Do You KNOW HOW?

Given $f(x) = 4x + 1$, describe how the graph of *g* compares with the graph of *f*.

5. $g(x) = 4(x + 3) + 1$

6. $g(x) = (4x + 1) + 3$

Given $f(x) = x + 2$, setting $k = 4$ affects the slope and *y*-intercept of the graph of *g* compared to the graph of *f*.

7. $g(x) = 4(x + 2)$

8. $g(x) = (4x) + 2$

9. The minimum wage for employees of a company is modeled by the function $f(x) = 7.25$. The company decided to offer a signing bonus of $75. How does adding this amount affect a graph of an employee's earnings?

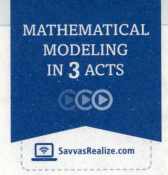
The Express Lane

Some supermarkets have self checkout lanes. Customers scan their items themselves and then pay with either cash or credit when they have finished scanning all of the items. Some customers think these lanes are faster than the checkout lanes with cashiers, but others don't like having to bag all of their purchases themselves.

What's your strategy for picking a checkout lane at the grocery store? Think about this during the Mathematical Modeling in 3 Acts lesson.

ACT 1 ▶ **Identify the Problem**

1. What is the first question that comes to mind after watching the video?

2. Write down the main question you will answer about what you saw in the video.

3. Make an initial conjecture that answers this main question.

4. Explain how you arrived at your conjecture.

5. What information will be useful to know to answer the main question? How can you get it? How will you use that information?

Video

ACT 2 **Develop a Model**

6. Use the math that you have learned in the topic to refine your conjecture.

ACT 3 **Interpret the Results**

7. Did your refined conjecture match the actual answer exactly? If not, what might explain the difference?

Go Online | SavvasRealize.com

3-4
Arithmetic Sequences

EXPLORE & REASON

A fashion designer is designing a patterned fabric.

Row Number

1 →
2 →
3 →
4 →
5 →

A. Copy and complete.

Row number	1	2	3	4	5
Number of Patterned Squares in the Row	1	▪	5	▪	▪
Total Number of Patterned Squares	1	▪	9	▪	▪

B. Use Structure What number patterns do you see in the rows of the table? © **MP.7**

HABITS OF MIND

Model with Mathematics What information would you need from the table to write a linear equation that represents the pattern? Explain. © **MP.4**

EXAMPLE 1   ☑ **Try It!** Connect Sequences and Functions

1. Is the domain of the function in Part B of Example 1 continuous or discrete? Explain.

EXAMPLE 2   ☑ **Try It!** Apply the Recursive Formula

2. Write a recursive formula to represent the total height of the nth stair above the ground if the height of each stair is 18 cm.

EXAMPLE 3   ☑ **Try It!** Apply the Explicit Formula

3. The cost to rent a bike is $28 for the first day plus $2 for each day after that. Write an explicit formula for the rental cost for n days. What is the cost of renting the bike for 8 days?

HABITS OF MIND

Reason Can a recursive formula have a negative common difference? Explain. Ⓒ **MP.2**

EXAMPLE 4   ☑ **Try It!** **Write an Explicit Formula From a Recursive Formula**

4. Write an explicit formula for each arithmetic sequence.

     a. $a_n = a_{n-1} - 3;\ a_1 = 10$ **b.** $a_n = a_{n-1} + 2.4;\ a_1 = -1$

EXAMPLE 5   ☑ **Try It!** **Write a Recursive Formula From an Explicit Formula**

5. Write a recursive formula for each explicit formula.

     a. $a_n = 8 + 3n$ **b.** $a_n = 12 - 5n$

HABITS OF MIND

Communicate Precisely Explain how you can use the recursive formula to find the value of any term in an arithmetic sequence. © **MP.6**

Do You UNDERSTAND?

1. ? **ESSENTIAL QUESTION** How are arithmetic sequences related to linear functions?

2. Error Analysis A student uses the explicit formula $a_n = 5 + 3(n - 1)$ for the sequence 3, 8, 13, 18, 23, ... to find the 12th term. Explain the error the student made. © **MP.3**

3. Vocabulary When is a *recursive formula* more useful than an *explicit formula* for an arithmetic sequence?

4. Communicate Precisely Compare and contrast a recursive formula and an explicit formula for an arithmetic sequence. © **MP.6**

Do You KNOW HOW?

Tell whether or not each sequence is an arithmetic sequence.

5. 15, 13, 11, 9, . . .

6. 4, 7, 10, 14, . . .

Write a recursive formula for each sequence.

7. 81, 85, 89, 93, 97, . . .

8. 47, 39, 31, 23, 15, . . .

9. An online store charges $5 to ship one box and $10 to ship two boxes. Write an explicit formula for an arithmetic sequence to represent the amount the online store charges to ship n boxes. Use the explicit formula to determine how much the online store charges when shipping 11 boxes.

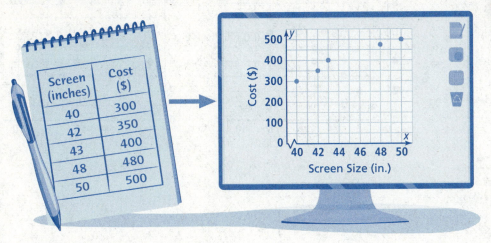
MODEL & DISCUSS

Nicholas plotted data points to represent the relationship between screen size and cost of television sets. Everything about the televisions is the same, except for the screen size.

Screen (inches)	Cost ($)
40	300
42	350
43	400
48	480
50	500

A. Describe any patterns you see.

B. What does this set of points tell you about the relationship of screen size and cost of the television?

C. Reason Where do you think the point for a 46-inch television would be on the graph? How about for a 60-inch TV? Explain. © MP.2

HABITS OF MIND

Use Appropriate Tools How can a table of values help determine whether data can be modeled by a linear function? © MP.5

Assess

EXAMPLE 1 ☑ Try It! Understand Association

1. Describe the type of association each scatter plot shows.

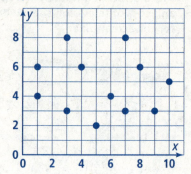

a.

b.

HABITS OF MIND

Reason What features of two data sets can help you determine whether the data sets have a negative, positive, or no association? © MP.2

EXAMPLE 2 ☑ Try It! Understand Correlation

2. How can the relationship between the hours after sunset *x* and the temperature *y* be modeled? If the relationship is modeled with a linear function, describe the correlation between the two data sets.

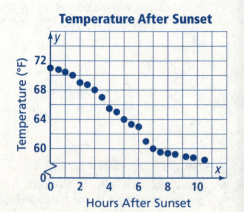

Temperature After Sunset

Hours After Sunset

📶 **Go Online** | SavvasRealize.com

EXAMPLE 3 ☑ **Try It!** **Write the Equation of a Trend Line**

3. a. What trend line, in slope-intercept form, models the data from the Example 2 Try It?

b. Explain why there could be no data points on a trend line, yet the line models the data.

EXAMPLE 4 ☑ **Try It!** **Interpret Trend Lines**

4. What is the x-intercept of the trend line? Is that possible in a real-world situation? Explain.

HABITS OF MIND

Construct Arguments What argument can you construct to defend a prediction based on a trend line? Explain. ⒸMP.3

Do You UNDERSTAND?

1. ? **ESSENTIAL QUESTION** How can you use a scatter plot to describe the relationship between two data sets?

2. Error Analysis A student claims that if *y*-values are not increasing as *x*-values increase, then the data must show a negative association. Explain the error the student made. © **MP.3**

3. Vocabulary In a scatter plot that shows *positive association*, describe how *y*-values change as *x*-values increase

4. Make Sense and Persevere Does a trend line need to pass through all the points in a scatter plot? Explain. © **MP.1**

5. Communicate Precisely Describe how the point-slope formula is useful when writing the equation for a trend line. © **MP.6**

Do You KNOW HOW?

Describe the type of association between *x* and *y* for each set of data. Explain.

6.

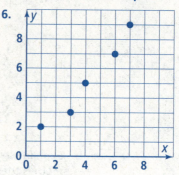

7.

x	4	6	7	9	10
y	9	7	5	3	3

8. The table shows the hours of studying *x* and a person's test score *y*. What is the equation of a trend line that models the data? What does the slope of your trend line represent?

Hours of Studying	0	1	1	2	3
Test Score	77	80	83	87	92

MODEL & DISCUSS

The scatter plot shows the number of beachgoers each day for the first six days of July. The head lifeguard at the beach uses the data to determine the number of lifeguards to schedule based on the weather forecast.

The head lifeguard compares two linear models:

$g(x) = 13x + 25$

$h(x) = 12x + 30$

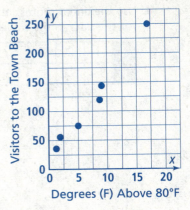

A. Copy the scatter plot and graph the linear functions on the same grid.

B. What is a reasonable domain for each function? Explain.

C. Construct Arguments Which model is the better predictor of the number of beachgoers based on the temperature above 80°F? Defend your model. © MP.3

HABITS OF MIND

Generalize Is there a limit to the number of lines that might be used to fit a set of points on a graph? Explain. © MP.8

EXAMPLE 1 **Try It!** **Find the Line of Best Fit**

1. Use the linear regression function to find the equation of the line of best fit for the data in the table.

x	1	2	4	5	7	8	9
y	5.4	6.1	8.1	8.5	10.3	10.9	11.5

EXAMPLE 2 **Try It!** **Understand Correlation Coefficients**

2. What does each correlation coefficient reveal about the data it describes?

   a. $r = 0.1$ b. $r = -0.6$

HABITS OF MIND

Communicate Precisely How are a strong negative correlation and a weak correlation different? Explain. Ⓒ **MP.6**

EXAMPLE 3   ☑ **Try It!** **Interpret Residual Plots**

3. The owner of Horizon Flight School also created a scatter plot and calculated the line of best fit for her enrollment data shown in the table. The equation of the line of best fit is $y = 1.44x + 877$. Find the residuals and plot them to determine how well this linear model fits the data.

Year (x)	0	1	2	3	4	5	6	7
Students (y)	832	872	905	928	903	887	863	867

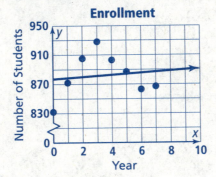

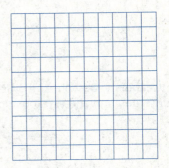

EXAMPLE 4   ☑ **Try It!** **Interpolate and Extrapolate Using Linear Models**

4. Using the model from Example 4, estimate the number of miles people flew on the airline in 2012.

EXAMPLE 5   ☑ **Try It!** **Correlation and Causation**

5. The number of cars in a number of cities shows a positive correlation to the population of the respective city. Can it be inferred that an increase of cars in a city leads to an increase in the population? Defend your response.

HABITS OF MIND

Construct Arguments What argument can you construct to explain why a given relationship would not be causal? Explain. ⒸMP.3

Do You UNDERSTAND?

1. ESSENTIAL QUESTION How can you evaluate the goodness of fit of a line of best fit for a paired data set?

2. Vocabulary Describe the difference between *interpolation* and *extrapolation*.

3. Error Analysis A student says that a correlation coefficient of −0.93 indicates that the two quantities of a data set have a weak correlation. Explain the error the student made. © MP.3

4. Look for Relationships A student found a strong correlation between the age of people who run marathons and their marathon time. Can the student say that young people will run marathons faster than older people? Explain. © MP.7

Do You KNOW HOW?

Use the table for Exercises 5 and 6.

x	10	20	30	40	50
y	7	11	14	20	22

5. Use technology to determine the equation of the line of best fit for the data.

6. Make a residual plot for the line of best fit and the data in the table. How well does the linear model fit the data?

7. The table shows the number of customers *y* at a store for *x* weeks after the store's grand opening. The equation for the line of best fit is $y = 7.77x + 38.8$. Assuming the trend continues, what is a reasonable prediction of the number of visitors to the store 7 weeks after its opening?

x	1	2	3	4	5	6
y	46	53	65	71	75	86

EXPLORE & REASON

Juan and Leo were supposed to meet and drive ATVs on a trail together. Juan is late so Leo started without him.

Leo
12 mi/h

The trail is 40 miles long.

Juan
15 mi/h

P

Not drawn to scale

A. Write an equation for Leo's distance from the starting point after riding for x hours. Write an equation for Juan's distance from the starting point if he starts h hours after Leo.

B. Model With Mathematics Suppose $h = 1$. How can you use graphs of the two equations to determine who finishes the trail first? **© MP.4**

C. How much of a head start must Leo have to finish the trail at the same time as Juan?

EXAMPLE 1 ☑ **Try It!** **Solve a System of Equations by Graphing**

1. Use a graph to solve each system of equations.

a. $\begin{cases} y = \frac{1}{2}x - 2 \\ y = 3x - 7 \end{cases}$

b. $\begin{cases} y = 2x + 10 \\ y = -\frac{1}{4}x + 1 \end{cases}$

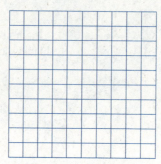
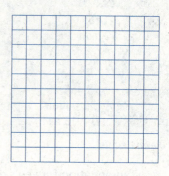

EXAMPLE 2 ☑ **Try It!** **Graph Systems of Equations With Infinitely Many or No Solutions**

2. Use a graph to solve each system of equations.

a. $\begin{cases} y = \frac{1}{2}x + 7 \\ 4x - 8y = 12 \end{cases}$

b. $\begin{cases} 3x + 2y = 9 \\ \frac{2}{3}y = 3 - x \end{cases}$

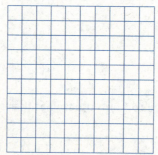
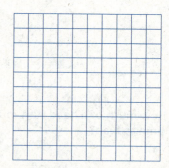

HABITS OF MIND

Reason Other than graphing, how else could you determine that an equation has infinitely many solutions? ⓒ **MP.2**

EXAMPLE 3 ☑ **Try It! Write a System of Equations**

3. Suppose Monisha reads 10 pages each day instead.

    a. How will that change the length of time it takes for Holly to catch up with Monisha?

    b. Will Holly still finish the novel first? Explain.

EXAMPLE 4 ☑ **Try It! Solve a System of Equations Approximately**

4. What solution do you obtain for the system of equations by graphing? What is the exact solution?

$$y = 5x - 4$$
$$y = -6x + 14$$

HABITS OF MIND

Use Appropriate Tools Holly and Monisha's classmate, Chris, is also finishing the novel. Chris has read 64 pages of the novel and plans to read 13 pages each day. When does Holly catch up to Chris? Does Chris finish the novel before Monisha? Ⓒ **MP.5**

Do You UNDERSTAND?

1. **ESSENTIAL QUESTION** How can you use a graph to illustrate the solution to a system of linear equations?

2. Model With Mathematics How does the graph of a system of equations with one solution differ from the graph of a system of equations with infinitely many solutions or no solution? © **MP.4**

3. Reason Why is the point of intersection for a system of equations considered its solution? © **MP.2**

4. Error Analysis Reese states that the system of equations has no solution because the slopes are the same. Describe Reese's error. © **MP.8**

$$y = -3x - 1$$
$$3x + y = -1$$

Do You KNOW HOW?

Solve each system of equations by graphing.

5. $y = 2x + 5$
$y = -\frac{1}{2}x$

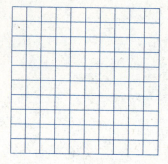

6. $y = -\frac{2}{3}x + 2$
$2x + 3y = 6$

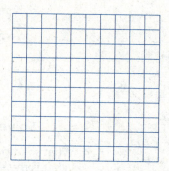

7. Juanita is painting her house. She can either buy Brand A paint and a paint roller tray or Brand B paint and a grid for the paint roller. For how many gallons of paint would the price for both options be the same? If Juanita needs 15 gallons of paint, which is the better option?

| 1-gallon can: $27/gallon | 1 paint roller tray: $3 | 1-gallon can: $25/gallon | 1 grid for paint roller: $5 |

MODEL & DISCUSS

Rochelle is conducting an experiment on cells of Elodea, a kind of water plant. To induce plasmolysis at the correct rate, she needs to use an 8% saline solution but she has only the solutions shown on hand.

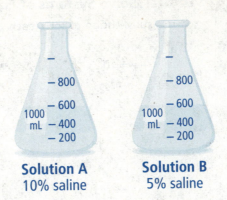

Solution A
10% saline

Solution B
5% saline

A. If Rochelle mixes the two solutions to get 1,000 mL of an 8% saline solution, which will she use more of? Explain.

B. How can Rochelle determine the amount of each solution she needs to make the 8% saline solution?

C. Use Appropriate Tools Are there any methods for solving this problem other than the one you used in part (b)? Explain. © **MP.5**

HABITS OF MIND
Look for Relationships Next, Rochelle wants to make 1,000 mL of a 7% saline solution. Would the amount of 10% solution in the 7% saline solution be more or less than the amount in the 8% saline solution? Explain. © **MP.7**

EXAMPLE 1   ☑ **Try It!** **Solve Systems of Equations Using Substitution**

1. Use substitution to solve each system of equations.

    a. $x = y + 6$
       $x + y = 10$

    b. $y = 2x - 1$
       $2x + 3y = -7$

EXAMPLE 2   ☑ **Try It!** **Compare Graphing and Substitution Methods**

2. On Saturday, the vacation resort offers a discount on water sports. To take a surfing lesson and go parasailing costs $130. That day, 25 people take surfing lessons, and 30 people go parasailing. A total of $3,650 is collected. What is the discounted price of each activity?

HABITS OF MIND

Generalize If you visit the vacation resort and find the cost of surfing lessons and parasailing by graphing the system of equations, what will you need to remember about the solution that you find? © **MP.8**

EXAMPLE 3   ☑ **Try It!** **Systems With Infinitely Many Solutions or No Solution**

3. Solve each system of equations.

a. $x + y = -4$
$y = -x + 5$

b. $y = -2x + 5$
$2x + y = 5$

EXAMPLE 4   ☑ **Try It!** **Model Using Systems of Equations**

4. Funtime Amusement Park charges $12.50 for admission and then $0.75 per ride. River's Edge Park charges $18.50 for admission and then $0.50 per ride. For what number of rides is the cost the same at both parks?

HABITS OF MIND

Make Sense and Persevere Healthy Start gym charges $32 for membership and then $6 per cycling class. Fast Fitness charges $29 for membership and then $6 per cycling class. Does a number of cycling classes exist for which the cost is the same at both gyms? © **MP.1**

Do You UNDERSTAND?

1. **ESSENTIAL QUESTION** How do you use substitution to solve a system of linear equations?

2. **Use Appropriate Tools** When is using a graph to solve a system of equations more useful than the substitution method? © MP.5

3. **Error Analysis** Simon solves a system of equations, in x and y, by substitution and gets an answer of $5 = 5$. He states that the solution to the system is all of the points (x, y) where x and y are real numbers. Describe Simon's error. © MP.3

4. **Use Structure** When solving a system of equations using substitution, how can you determine whether the system has one solution, no solution, or infinitely many solutions? © MP.7

Do You KNOW HOW?

Use substitution to solve each system of equations.

5. $y = 6 - x$
   $4x - 3y = -4$

6. $x = -y + 3$
   $3x - 2y = -1$

7. $-3x - y = 7$
   $x + 2y = 6$

8. $6x - 3y = -6$
   $y = 2x + 2$

9. A sports store sells a total of 70 soccer balls in one month, and collects a total of $2,400. Write and solve a system of equations to determine how many of each type of soccer ball were sold.

Limited Edition soccer ball $65.00	Pro NSL soccer ball $15.00

CRITIQUE & EXPLAIN

Sadie and Micah used different methods to solve the system of equations.

$$y = 2x + 3$$
$$4x - y = 5$$

SavvasRealize.com

Sadie's work

$$4x - (2x + 3) = 5$$
$$4x - 2x - 3 = 5$$
$$2x - 3 = 5$$
$$2x = 8$$
$$x = 4$$
$$y = 2(4) + 3 = 11$$

The solution is (4, 11).

Micah's work

$$y = 2x + 3 \text{ and } y = 4x - 5$$
$$2x + 3 = 4x - 5$$
$$8 = 2x$$
$$x = 4$$
$$y = 2(4) + 3$$
$$y = 11$$

The solution is (4, 11).

A. In what ways are Sadie's and Micah's approaches similar? In what ways are they different?

B. Are both Sadie's and Micah's approaches valid solution methods? Explain.

C. Reason Which method of solving systems of equations do you prefer when solving, Sadie's method, or Micah's method? Explain. © **MP.2**

HABITS OF MIND

Reason Can you think of an instance when it is more convenient to use Sadie's method? When is it more convenient to use Micah's method? © **MP.2**

EXAMPLE 1 ✓ **Try It!** Solve a System of Equations by Adding

1. Solve each system of equations.

a. $2x - 4y = 2$
$-x + 4y = 3$

b. $2x + 3y = 1$
$-2x + 2y = -6$

EXAMPLE 2 ✓ **Try It!** Understand Equivalent Systems of Equations

2. Solve each system of equations.

a. $x + 2y = 4$
$2x - 5y = -1$

b. $2x + y = 2$
$x - 2y = -5$

- - - - - - - - - - - - -

HABITS OF MIND

Look for Relationships How could you write an equivalent system of equations for both of the systems in Try It! 2? © **MP.7**

EXAMPLE 3   ☑ **Try It!** **Apply Elimination**

3. Before the florist has a chance to finish the bouquets, a large order is placed. After the order, only 85 roses and 163 peonies remain. How many regular bouquets and mini bouquets can the florist make now?

EXAMPLE 4   ☑ **Try It!** **Choose a Method of Solving**

4. What is the solution of each system of equations? Explain your choice of solution method.

   a. $6x + 12y = -6$
       $3x - 2y = -27$

   b. $3x - 2y = 38$
       $x = 6 - y$

HABITS OF MIND

Communicate Precisely Explain the difference between solving a system of equations using substitution and solving a system of equations using elimination. ⓒ **MP.6**

Do You UNDERSTAND?

1. **ESSENTIAL QUESTION** Why does the elimination method work when solving a system of equations?

2. **Error Analysis** Esteban tries to solve the following system.

$7x - 4y = -12$

$x - 2y = 4$

His first step is to multiply the second equation by 3.

$7x - 4y = -12$

$3x - 6y = 12$

Then he adds the equations to eliminate a term. What is Esteban's error? © **MP.3**

3. **Construct Arguments** How can you determine whether two systems of equations are equivalent? © **MP.3**

4. **Mathematical Connections** The sum of 5 times the width of a rectangle and twice its length is 26 units. The difference of 15 times the width and three times the length is 6 units. Write and solve a system of equations to find the length and width of the rectangle.

Do You KNOW HOW?

Solve each system of equations.

5. $4x - 2y = -2$
   $3x + 2y = -12$

6. $3x + 2y = 4$
   $3x + 6y = -24$

7. $4x - 3y = -9$
   $3x + 2y = -11$

8. $x - 3y = -4$
   $2x - 6y = 6$

9. Ella is a landscape photographer. One weekend at her gallery she sells a total of 52 prints for a total of $2,975. How many of each size print did Ella sell?

Small print: $50   Large print: $75

MODEL & DISCUSS

A flatbed trailer carrying a load can have a maximum total height of 13 feet, 6 inches. The photograph shows the height of the trailer before a load is placed on top. What are the possible heights of loads that could be carried on the trailer?

5 ft

4-4
Linear Inequalities in Two Variables

A. What type of model could represent this situation? Explain.

B. Will the type of model you chose show all the possible heights of the loads without going over the maximum height? Explain.

C. Reason Interpret the solutions of the model. How many solutions are there? Explain. © MP.2

HABITS OF MIND

Make Sense and Persevere Suppose that the maximum load is transferred to a different flat bed. If the new flat bed has a maximum total height of 14 feet, what should the height of the new load on the flatbed be to ensure the flatbed and the load do not exceed the maximum total height? © MP.1

EXAMPLE 1   ☑ **Try It!** Understand an Inequality in Two Variables

1. Describe the graph of the solutions of each inequality.

   a. $y < -3x + 5$.

   b. $y \geq -3x + 5$

EXAMPLE 2   ☑ **Try It!** Rewrite an Inequality to Graph It

2. Will the Science Club meet their goal if they sell 30 T-shirts and 90 key chains? Explain in terms of the graph of the inequality.

HABITS OF MIND

Communicate Precisely How is the graph of $y < 3x$ similar to the graph of $y \geq 3x$? How are the two graphs different? ⒸMP.6

EXAMPLE 3 ☑ Try It! Write an Inequality From a Graph

3. What inequality does each graph represent?

a.

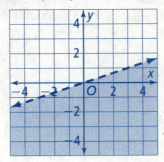

b.

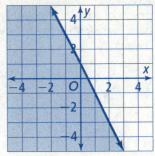

EXAMPLE 4 ☑ Try It! Inequalities in One Variable in the Coordinate Plane

4. Graph each inequality in the coordinate plane.

a. $y > -2$

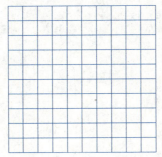

b. $x \leq 1$

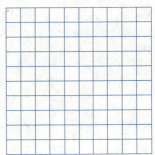

HABITS OF MIND

Use Appropriate Tools Name two ways you could check if a point is a solution of an inequality. Ⓒ MP.5

Do You UNDERSTAND?

1. **ESSENTIAL QUESTION** How does the graph of a linear inequality in two variables help you identify the solutions of the inequality?

2. Communicate Precisely How many solutions does a linear inequality in two variables have? **© MP.6**

3. Vocabulary In what form do you write one of the *solutions of an inequality in two variables*?

4. Error Analysis A student claims that the inequality $y < 1$ cannot be graphed on a coordinate grid since it has only one variable. Explain the error the student made. **© MP.3**

Do You KNOW HOW?

Tell whether each ordered pair is a solution of the inequality $y > x + 1$.

5. (0, 1)

6. (3, 5)

Graph each inequality in the coordinate plane.

7. $y \geq 2x$

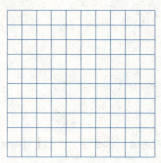

8. $y < x - 2$

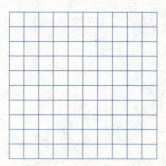

9. What inequality is shown by the graph?

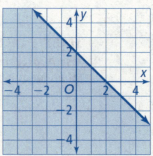

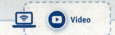
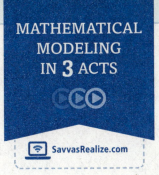

Get Up There!

Have you ever been to the top of a skyscraper? If so, you probably didn't take the stairs. You probably took an elevator. How long did it take you to get to the top? Did you take an express elevator?

Express elevators travel more quickly because they do not stop at every floor. How much more quickly can you get to the top in an express elevator? Think about this during the Mathematical Modeling in 3 Acts lesson.

ACT 1

1. What is the first question that comes to mind after watching the video?

2. Write down the main question you will answer about what you saw in the video.

3. Make an initial conjecture that answers this main question.

4. Explain how you arrived at your conjecture.

5. What information will be useful to know to answer the main question? How can you get it? How will you use that information?

ACT 2

6. Use the math that you have learned in the topic to refine your conjecture.

ACT 3

7. Did your refined conjecture match the actual answer exactly? If not, what might explain the difference?

 Activity

⏻ EXPLORE & REASON

The graph shows the equations $y = x - 1$ and $y = -2x + 4$.

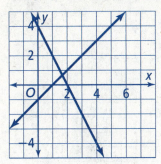

A. Choose some points above and below the line $y = x - 1$. Which of them are solutions to $y > x - 1$? Which are solutions to $y < x - 1$?

B. Choose some points above and below the line $y = -2x + 4$. Which of them are solutions to $y > -2x + 4$? Which are solutions to $y < -2x + 4$?

C. **Look for Relationships** The two lines divide the plane into four regions. How can you describe each region in terms of the inequalities in parts A and B? © MP.7

- -

HABITS OF MIND

Reason Are points on the line part of any of the four regions described in Part C? Explain. © MP.2

EXAMPLE 1   ☑ **Try It!** **Graph a System of Inequalities**

    1. Graph each system of inequalities.

    a. $y < 2x$
       $y > -3$

    b. $y \geq -2x + 1$
       $y > x + 2$

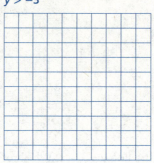
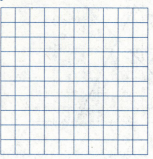

EXAMPLE 2   ☑ **Try It!** **Write a System of Inequalities From a Graph**

    2. What system of inequalities is shown by each graph?

    a.
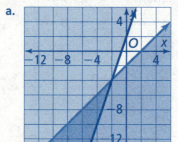

    b.
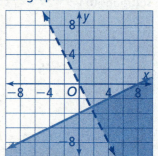

HABITS OF MIND

Use Appropriate Tools What would the graph of a system of inequalities with no solutions look like? ⓒ **MP.5**

EXAMPLE 3   ☑ **Try It!** **Use a System of Inequalities**

3. Use the graph in Example 3 to determine if Malia can buy 75 water bottles and 100 pairs of socks. Explain.

HABITS OF MIND

Generalize What do the nonoverlapping portions of the shaded regions represent? © MP.8

Do You UNDERSTAND?

1. **ESSENTIAL QUESTION** How is the graph of a system of linear inequalities related to the solutions of the system of inequalities?

2. Error Analysis A student say that (0, 1) is a solution to the following system of inequalities.

$$y > x$$
$$y > 2x + 1$$

She says that (0, 1) is a solution because it is a solution of $y > x$. Explain the error that the student made. Ⓒ **MP.3**

3. Vocabulary How many inequalities are in a *system of inequalities*?

4. Use Appropriate Tools Is it easier to describe the solution of a system of linear inequalities in words or to show it using a graph? Explain. Ⓒ **MP.5**

Do You KNOW HOW?

Identify the boundary lines for each system of inequalities.

5. $y > -3x + 4$
   $y \leq 8x + 1$

6. $y < -6x$
   $y \geq 10x - 3$

Graph each system of inequalities.

7. $y \leq -3x$
   $y < 2$

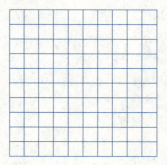

8. $y \geq x - 4$
   $y < -x$

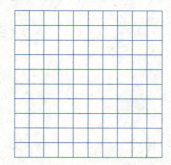

9. What system of inequalities is shown by the graph?

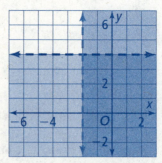

EXPLORE & REASON

Groups of students are hiking from mile markers 2, 6 and 8 to meet at the waterfall located at mile marker 5.

A. How can you use the mile marker to determine the number of miles each group of students needs to hike to the waterfall?

B. **Model With Mathematics** Make a graph that relates the position of each group on the trail to their distance from the waterfall. Ⓒ **MP.4**

C. How would the points in your graph from part B change as the groups of students approach the waterfall?

HABITS OF MIND

Reason Why is the absolute value of a number always positive? How does it relate to real-world situations? Explain. Ⓒ **MP.2**

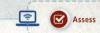
EXAMPLE 1 ☑ **Try It!** **Graph the Absolute Value Function**

1. What are the domain and range of $f(x) = |x|$?

EXAMPLE 2 ☑ **Try It!** **Transform the Absolute Value Function**

2. How do the domain and range of each function compare with the domain and range of $f(x) = |x|$?

a. $g(x) = \frac{1}{2}|x|$

b. $h(x) = -2|x|$

HABITS OF MIND

Generalize Are there statements you can make about the domain of $f(x) = a|x|$ that are always true? Explain. ⓒ **MP.8**

EXAMPLE 3 ☑ **Try It!** **Interpret the Graph of a Function**

3. A cyclist competing in a race rides past a water station. The graph of the function $d(t) = \frac{1}{3}|t - 60|$ shows her distance from the water station at t minutes. Assume the graph represents the entire race. What does the graph tell you about her race?

EXAMPLE 4 ☑ **Try It!** **Determine Rate of Change**

4. Kata gets on a moving walkway at the airport. Then 8 s after she gets on, she taps Lisa, who is standing alongside the walkway. The graph shows Kata's distance from Lisa over time. Calculate the rate of change in her distance from Lisa from 6 s to 8 s, and then from 8 s to 12 s. What do the rates of change mean in terms of Kata's movement?

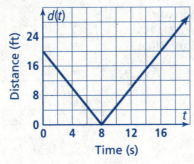

HABITS OF MIND

Make Sense and Persevere If a function that includes an absolute value expression represents a real-world distance situation, what is the vertex of the graph likely to represent? Explain. ⓒ **MP.1**

☑ Do You UNDERSTAND?

1. **?** ESSENTIAL QUESTION What are the key features of the graph of the absolute value function?

2. **Communicate Precisely** How do the domain and range of $g(x) = a|x|$ compare to the domain and range of $f(x) = |x|$ when $0 < a < 1$? Explain. Ⓒ **MP.6**

3. **Make Sense and Persevere** The graph of the function $g(x) = a|x|$ includes the point (1, 16). What is another point on the function? What is the value of a? Ⓒ **MP.1**

4. **Error Analysis** Janiece says that the vertex of the graph of $g(x) = a|x|$ always represents the minimum value of the function g. Explain her error. Ⓒ **MP.3**

Do You KNOW HOW?

Find the domain and range of each function.

5. $g(x) = 5|x|$

6. $h(x) = -2|x|$

Graph each function.

7. $g(x) = 1.5|x|$

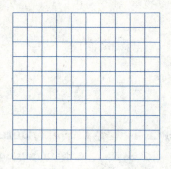

8. $h(x) = -0.8|x|$

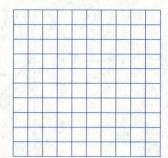

9. What is the rate of change over the interval $15 \le x \le 18$?

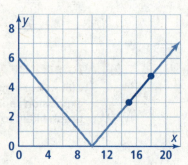

Go Online | SavvasRealize.com

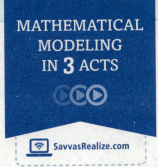

The Mad Runner

People run in many different places: on the soccer field during a game, around the neighborhood, on the basketball court, on the street to catch a bus, in gym class.

Sometimes people run on flat ground and other times they run up or down hills or even up and down stairs. They also run on different surfaces, such as grass, pavement, sand, or a basketball court. Think about this during the Mathematical Modeling in 3 Acts lesson.

ACT 1 ▶ Identify the Problem

1. What is the first question that comes to mind after watching the video?

2. Write down the Main Question you will answer about what you saw in the video.

ACT 2 ▶ Identify the Problem

3. Make a graph that represents this situation.

ACT 3 ▶ Interpret the Results

4. Did your graph match the actual answer exactly? If not, what might explain the difference?

EXPLORE & REASON

In a relay race, each runner carries a baton for an equal distance, with each runner handing off the baton to the next runner.

Path of the Baton

	Time (min)	Total Distance (mi)
Start	0	0
Runner 1	3	0.25
Runner 2	5.75	0.50
Runner 3	9	0.75
Runner 4	11.50	1.00

A. Graph the distance traveled by the baton as a function of time. How is the speed of each runner represented in the graph?

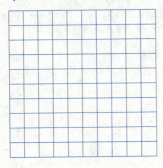

B. Who is the fastest runner?

C. **Communicate Precisely** How is the graph of this function similar to the graph of a linear function? How is it different? © MP.6

HABITS OF MIND

Use Appropriate Tools How does making a graph help you understand the function and the situation? Explain. © MP.5

EXAMPLE 1 ☑ **Try It!** **Understand Piecewise-Defined Functions**

1. Express $f(x) = -3|x|$ as a piecewise-defined function.

EXAMPLE 2 ☑ **Try It!** **Graph a Piecewise-Defined Function**

2. Graph the following function. $f(x) = \begin{cases} x - 2, & x \le 1 \\ -2x + 3, & x > 1 \end{cases}$

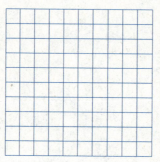

HABITS OF MIND

Communicate Precisely How does the domain of the function relate to the piecewise-defined function notation? ⓒ **MP.6**

Go Online | SavvasRealize.com

EXAMPLE 3　　☑ **Try It!** **Analyze the Graph of a Piecewise-Defined Function**

3. Make a conjecture about why a utility company might charge higher rates for greater levels of water consumption.

EXAMPLE 4　　☑ **Try It!** **Apply a Piecewise-Defined Function**

4. What is the difference in cost between one order of 200 wristbands, two orders of 100 wristbands each, and four orders of 50 wristbands each?

HABITS OF MIND

Look for Relationships How can you tell when the pieces of a piecewise-defined function do not connect? Explain. ⓒ **MP.7**

☑ Do You UNDERSTAND?

1. ❓ **ESSENTIAL QUESTION** What are the key features of piecewise-defined functions?

2. **Construct Arguments** If the domain of a piecewise-defined function f is all real numbers, must the range of f also be all real numbers? Explain. ⓒ **MP.3**

3. **Error Analysis** Liz wrote the following piecewise-defined function:

$$f(x) = \begin{cases} x - 3, & x \le -3 \\ -2x - 4, & x \ge -3 \end{cases}$$

What is the error that Liz made? ⓒ **MP.3**

4. **Reason** How many pieces does the absolute value function have? Explain. ⓒ **MP.2**

Do You KNOW HOW?

Express each function as a piecewise-defined function.

5. $f(x) = 5|x|$

6. $f(x) = -2|x|$

Graph each function.

7. $f(x) = \begin{cases} -3x + 1, & x \le 1 \\ x + 1, & x > 1 \end{cases}$

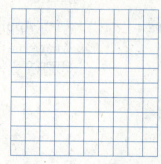

8. $f(x) = \begin{cases} 2x - 1, & x < 3 \\ -2x + 4, & x \ge 3 \end{cases}$

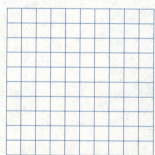

9. A function f is defined by the rule $-0.5x + 1$ for the domain $x < 1$ and by the rule x for the domain $x \ge 1$. Write the piecewise-defined function f using function notation.

CRITIQUE & EXPLAIN

Students are told there is a function where decimals are the inputs and each decimal is rounded to the nearest whole number to get the output. Beth and Latoya each make a sketch of the graph of the function.

 SavvasRealize.com

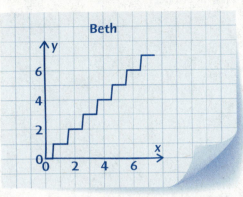

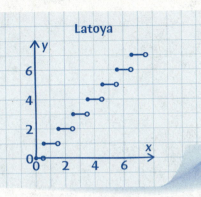

A. **Make Sense and Persevere** What is causing both students to create graphs that look like steps? © MP.1

B. Which graph do you think is correct? Explain.

C. What does the graph of this function look like? Explain.

EXAMPLE 1 ☑ **Try It!** **Understand Step Functions**

1. Evaluate each function for the given value.

    a. $f(x) = \lceil x \rceil$; $x = 2.65$

    b. $f(x) = \text{floor}(x)$; $x = 2.19$

HABITS OF MIND

Look for Relationships Why are the graphs of floor and ceiling functions composed of horizontal sections? ⓒ **MP.7**

EXAMPLE 2   ☑ **Try It!** **Use a Step Function to Represent a Real-World Situation**

2. The postage for a first-class letter weighing one ounce or less is $0.47. Each additional ounce is $0.21. The maximum weight of a first-class letter is $3\frac{1}{2}$ oz. Write a function to represent the situation.

EXAMPLE 3   ☑ **Try It!** **Use a Step Function**

3. You rent a karaoke machine at 1 P.M. and plan to return it by 4 P.M. Will you save any money if you return the machine 15 min early? Explain.

HABITS OF MIND

Model With Mathematics Why are ceiling functions useful in modeling real-world situations? ⒸMP.4

☑ Do You UNDERSTAND?

1. 🅠 **ESSENTIAL QUESTION** How are step functions related to piecewise-defined functions?

2. Vocabulary How are the *ceiling function* and the *floor function* similar? How are they different?

3. Error Analysis Jason defined the following step function.

$$f(x) = \begin{cases} 5, 0 \le x \le 10 \\ 6, 10 \le x \le 20 \\ 7, 20 \le x \le 30 \end{cases}$$

What is the error that Jason made? © MP.3

4. Reason For the function that rounds numbers to the nearest whole number, what are the pieces of the domain for the interval from 0 to 4? © MP.2

Do You KNOW HOW?

Evaluate the ceiling function for the given value.

5. $f(x) = \lceil x \rceil$; $x = 5.13$

6. $f(x) = \text{ceiling}(x)$; $x = 11.71$

Evaluate the floor function for the given value.

7. $f(x) = \lfloor x \rfloor$; $x = 9.37$

8. $f(x) = \text{floor}(x)$; $x = 5.49$

9. Graph the function f.

x	f(x)
$0 < x \le 1$	4
$1 < x \le 2$	5
$2 < x \le 3$	6
$3 < x \le 4$	7
$4 < x \le 5$	8
$5 < x \le 6$	9

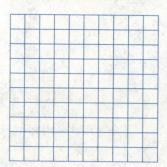

MODEL & DISCUSS

Cleo takes three 1-hour classes at a community college. The graph shows the time she spends in each class.

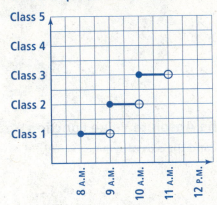

A. Next semester, each class will start an hour later. How will this change the graph?

B. How will the graph change if she takes two 90-minute classes, one starting at 8:30 A.M. and the second at 10:00 A.M.?

C. **Construct Arguments** Starting in the fall, Cleo will take three classes in a row with the first starting at 7:00 A.M. Cleo says that she can update the graph by moving all three steps one unit to the left. Do you agree? Justify your answer. **© MP.3**

HABITS OF MIND

Look for Relationships What have you learned about graphing functions that is useful in analyzing this problem? **© MP.7**

EXAMPLE 1 ☑ **Try It!** **Translate Step Functions**

1. How will the total points awarded for a $1.25 juice drink change if the bonus points are decreased by 2 points?

EXAMPLE 2 ☑ **Try It!** **Vertical Translations of the Absolute Value Function**

2. For each function, identify the vertex and the axis of symmetry.

   a. $p(x) = |x| + 3$

   b. $g(x) = |x| - 2$

HABITS OF MIND

Generalize What did you notice about the equations of step and absolute value functions that result in vertical translations? © **MP.8**

EXAMPLE 3   **Try It!** **Horizontal Translations of the Absolute Value Function**

3. For each function, identify the vertex and the axis of symmetry.

   a. $g(x) = |x - 3|$

   b. $p(x) = |x + 5|$

EXAMPLE 4 ☑ **Try It!** **Understand Vertical and Horizontal Translations**

4. Find the vertex of the graph of each function.

   a. $g(x) = |x - 1| - 3$

   b. $g(x) = |x + 2| + 6$

HABITS OF MIND

Reason How is the algebraic representation of a function that translates the graph of $f(x) = |x|$ horizontally different from one that translates the graph of f vertically? Ⓒ **MP.2**

EXAMPLE 5 ☑ **Try It!** **Understand Vertical Stretches and Compressions**

5. Compare the graph of each function with the graph of $f(x) = |x|$.

   a. $g(x) = 3|x|$ b. $g(x) = -\frac{1}{3}|x|$

EXAMPLE 6 ☑ **Try It!** **Understand Transformations of the Absolute Value Function**

6. a. Write a function for the graph shown.

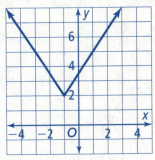

   b. Write the function of the graph after a translation 1 unit right and 4 units up.

HABITS OF MIND

Use Structure How can you use the symmetric structure of the graph of $g(x) = a|x - h| + k$ to help you graph the function? Explain. Ⓒ **MP.7**

✓ Do You UNDERSTAND?

1. ❓ ESSENTIAL QUESTION How do the constants affect the graphs of piecewise-defined functions?

2. Generalize How do the constants a, h, and k affect the domain and range of $g(x) = a|x - h| + k$ when $a > 0$? ⓒ MP.8

3. Error Analysis Jacy says that $f(x) = 4|x - 1|$ and $f(x) = |4x - 1|$ have the same graph. Is Jacy correct? Explain. ⓒ MP.3

4. Use Structure How can you reflect the graph of $f(x) = 3|x + 2| + 1$ across the x-axis? ⓒ MP.7

Do You KNOW HOW?

Find the vertex and graph each function.

5. $f(x) = |x| + 2.5$

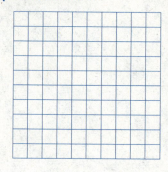

6. $f(x) = |x + 2.5|$

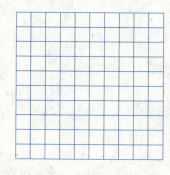

7. $f(x) = |x - 2| + 4$

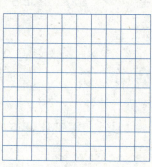

8. $f(x) = -3|x + 1| - 5$

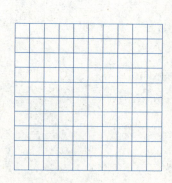

9. What is the equation of the graph?

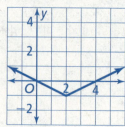

CRITIQUE & EXPLAIN

Students are asked to write an equivalent expression for 3^{-3}. Casey and Jacinta each write an expression on the board.

Casey

$3^{-3} = -27$

Jacinta

$3^{-3} = \dfrac{1}{27}$

A. Who is correct, Casey or Jacinta? Explain.

B. Reason What is the most likely error that was made? © **MP.2**

HABITS OF MIND

Look for Relationships How do you know when exponential expressions are equivalent? Explain. © **MP.7**

EXAMPLE 1 ☑ **Try It!** **Write Radicals Using Rational Exponents**

1. What does $2^{\frac{1}{3}}$ equal? Explain.

EXAMPLE 2 ☑ **Try It!** **Use the Product of Powers Property to Solve Equations With Rational Exponents**

2. What is the solution of $\left(2^{\frac{x}{4}}\right)\left(2^{\frac{x}{6}}\right) = 2^3$?

EXAMPLE 3 ☑ **Try It!** **Use the Power of Power Property to Solve Equations With Rational Exponents**

3. What is the solution of each equation?

　　a. $256^{x+2} = 4^{3x+9}$

　　b. $\left(\frac{1}{8}\right)^{\frac{x}{2}-1} = \left(\frac{1}{4}\right)^{\frac{x}{3}}$

HABITS OF MIND

Communicate Precisely When is the value of an expression undefined? Explain. ⒸMP.6

EXAMPLE 4 ☑ **Try It!** **Use the Power of a Product Property to Solve Equations With Rational Exponents**

4. When the side length of Blanket A is multiplied by $2^{\frac{1}{2}}$ the result is 6 yards. Find the area of Blanket A.

EXAMPLE 5 ☑ **Try It!** **Use the Quotient of Powers Property to Solve Equations With Rational Exponents**

5. What is the value of x if the side length of Terrarium A is 3 times greater than the side length of Terrarium B?

HABITS OF MIND

Look for Relationships Can you use the same properties of exponents for expressions with rational exponents as you do when computing with integers? Explain. © MP.7

Do You UNDERSTAND?

1. **ESSENTIAL QUESTION** What are the properties of rational exponents and how are they used to solve problems?

2. **Communicate Precisely** A square has an area of 15 ft². What are two ways of expressing its side lengths? Ⓒ **MP.6**

3. **Look for Relationships** If $3^x = 3^y$, what is the relationship between x and y? Ⓒ **MP.7**

4. **Error Analysis** Corey wrote $\sqrt[3]{4^2}$ as $4^{\frac{3}{2}}$. What error did Corey make? Ⓒ **MP.3**

5. **Reason** When is it useful to have rational exponents instead of radicals? Ⓒ **MP.2**

6. **Vocabulary** How are *rational exponents* different than whole number exponents? How are they the same?

Do You KNOW HOW?

Write each radical using rational exponents.

7. $\sqrt{7}$

8. $\sqrt{15}$

9. $\sqrt[3]{6^4}$

10. $\sqrt[3]{2^3}$

11. $\sqrt[4]{2^4}$

12. $\sqrt{8^3}$

Solve each equation.

13. $\left(2^{\frac{x}{3}}\right)\left(2^{\frac{x}{4}}\right) = 2^5$

14. $\left(4^{\frac{x}{2}}\right)\left(4^{\frac{x}{5}}\right) = 4^8$

15. $64^{x+1} = 4^{x+7}$

16. $16^{(x-3)} = 2^{(x-6)}$

17. $\left(\frac{1}{243}\right)^{-\frac{x}{3}} = \left(\frac{1}{9}\right)^{-\frac{x}{2}+1}$

18. $\left(\frac{1}{36}\right)^{(x-4)} = \left(\frac{1}{216}\right)^{x+1}$

EXPLORE & REASON

Use two pieces of $8\frac{1}{2}$ by 11 paper. Fold one of the pieces of paper accordion-style for five folds. Fold the other in half for five folds. After each fold, unfold each piece of paper and count the total number of rectangular sections.

Accordion-Style Folds

Half Folds

A. Find the pattern relating the number of folds to the number of sections for each folding style. What do you notice?

B. Make Sense and Persevere Explain why the two different folded pieces of paper produce different results. © **MP.1**

HABITS OF MIND

Model With Mathematics Describe another situation that you could represent using an exponential function. © **MP.4**

EXAMPLE 1   ☑ **Try It!** **Key Features of Exponential Functions**

1. Identify the key features of the function $f(x) = b^x$ for $b = 2$ and $b = \frac{1}{2}$ similar.

EXAMPLE 2   ☑ **Try It!** **Graph Exponential Functions**

2. How long will it take for the virus to spread to 50,000 computers?

HABITS OF MIND

Use Appropriate Tools Suppose the spread of another virus is modeled by the function $g(x) = 5^x$. If it takes the virus five and a half hours to spread, what tools could you use to investigate the function $g(x) = 5^x$? © **MP.5**

EXAMPLE 3 ☑ **Try It!** **Write Exponential Functions**

3. Write an exponential function for each set of points.

    a. (0, 3), (1, 12), (2, 48), (3, 192), and (4, 768)

    b. (0, 2,187), (1, 729), (2, 243), (3, 81), and (4, 27)

EXAMPLE 4 ☑ **Try It!** **Compare Linear and Exponential Functions**

4. Identify each function as linear or exponential. Explain.

    a. $f(x)$ equals the number of branches at level x in a tree diagram, where at each level each branch extends into 4 branches.

    b. $f(x)$ equals the number of boxes in row x of a stack in which each row increases by 2 boxes.

HABITS OF MIND

Use Structure In an exponential function, why is a a nonzero constant and $b \neq 1$? Ⓒ **MP.7**

Do You UNDERSTAND?

1. **ESSENTIAL QUESTION** What are the characteristics of exponential functions?

2. **Look for Relationships** How can you tell whether the graph of a function of form $f(x) = ab^x$, where $a > 0$, will increase or decrease from left to right? © **MP.7**

3. **Make Sense and Persevere** Why is $b \neq 1$ a condition for $f(x) = ab^x$? © **MP.1**

4. **Error Analysis** Martin says that $f(x) = 2(4)^x$ starts at 4 and has constant ratio of 2. What error did Martin make? Explain. © **MP.3**

Do You KNOW HOW?

Graph each function.

5. $f(x) = 3^x$

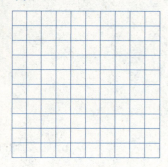

6. $f(x) = \left(\frac{1}{4}\right)^x$

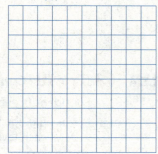

Write each exponential function.

7.

x	f(x)
0	4
1	2
2	1
3	$\frac{1}{2}$
4	$\frac{1}{4}$

8.

x	f(x)
0	3
1	6
2	12
3	24
4	48

EXPLORE & REASON

Cindy is buying a new car and wants to learn how the value of her car will change over time. Insurance actuaries predict the future value of cars using depreciation functions. One such function is applied to the car whose declining value is shown.

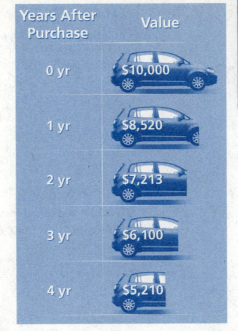

Years After Purchase	Value
0 yr	$10,000
1 yr	$8,520
2 yr	$7,213
3 yr	$6,100
4 yr	$5,210

A. Describe how the value of the car decreases from year to year.

B. Model With Mathematics What kind of function would explain this type of pattern? © MP.4

C. Given your answer to Part B, what is needed to find the function the actuary is using? Explain.

HABITS OF MIND

Make Sense and Persevere What is the constant ratio for the declining values? © MP.1

EXAMPLE 1   ☑ **Try It!** **Exponential Growth**

1. The population of Valleytown is also 5,000, with an annual increase of 1,000. Can the expected population for Valleytown be modeled with an exponential growth function? Explain.

EXAMPLE 2   ☑ **Try It!** **Exponential Models of Growth**

2. a. What will be the difference after 15 years if the interest is compounded semiannually rather than quarterly?

b. What would be the difference in after 15 years if the interest is compounded monthly rather than quarterly?

HABITS OF MIND

Communicate Precisely Explain why the total value increases the more times a value is compounded. Ⓒ **MP.6**

EXAMPLE 3   ☑ **Try It!** **Exponential Decay**

3. Suppose the number of views decreases by 20% per day. In how many days will the number of views per day be less than 1,000?

EXAMPLE 4 ☑ **Try It! Exponential Models of Decay**

4. How would the average rate of change over the same intervals be affected if the population increased at a rate of 8%?

EXAMPLE 5 ☑ **Try It! Exponential Growth and Decay**

5. Explain how to use tables on a graphing calculator to answer this question.

HABITS OF MIND

Model With Mathematics What are the key differences in the algebraic representations of exponential growth and decay? Explain. ⓒ **MP.4**

Do You UNDERSTAND?

1. **ESSENTIAL QUESTION** What kinds of situations can be modeled with exponential growth or exponential decay?

2. **Vocabulary** What is the difference between simple interest and *compound interest*?

3. **Error Analysis** LaTanya says that the growth factor of $f(x) = 100(1.25)^x$ is 25%. What mistake did LaTanya make? Explain. Ⓒ **MP.3**

4. **Look for Relationships** Why is the growth factor $1 + r$ for an exponential growth function? Ⓒ **MP.7**

Do You KNOW HOW?

Write an exponential growth or decay function for each situation.

5. initial value of 100 increasing at a rate of 5%

6. initial value of 1,250 increasing at a rate of 25%

7. initial value of 512 decreasing at a rate of 50%

8. initial value of 10,000 decreasing at a rate of 12%

9. What is the difference in the value after 10 years of an initial investment of $2,000 at 5% annual interest when the interest is compounded quarterly rather than annually?

6-4
Geometric Sequences

EXPLORE & REASON

A seating plan is being designed for Section 12 of a new stadium.

Row E
Row D
Row C
Row B
Row A

A. Describe the pattern.

B. Write an equation for this pattern.

C. Use Structure Row Z of Section 12 must have at least 75 seats. If the pattern continues, does this seating plan meet that requirement? Justify your answer. Ⓒ **MP.7**

HABITS OF MIND

Use Appropriate Tools When is using a diagram the best tool to determine the number of seats in a given row? Explain. Ⓒ **MP.1**

EXAMPLE 1 ☑ **Try It!** **Identify Arithmetic and Geometric Sequences**

1. Is each sequence an arithmetic or a geometric sequence? Explain.

   a. 1, 2.2, 4.84, 10.648, 23.4256, ...

   b. 1, 75, 149, 223, 297, ...

EXAMPLE 2 ☑ **Try It!** **Write the Recursive Formula For a Sequence**

2. Write the recursive formulas for the geometric sequence 3,072, 768, 192, 48, 12, ...

HABITS OF MIND

Make Sense and Persevere Explain why a common ratio in a geometric sequence cannot be zero. Ⓒ **MP.1**

EXAMPLE 3 ☑ **Try It!** **Use the Explicit Formula**

3. What is the 12th term of the sequence described?
Initial condition is 3
recursive formula is $a_n = 6(a_{n-1})$

EXAMPLE 4 ✓ **Try It!** **Connect Geometric Sequences and Exponential Functions**

4. How many subscribers will there be in Week 9 if the initial number of subscribers is 10?

EXAMPLE 5 ✓ **Try It!** **Apply the Recursive and Explicit Formulas**

5. The formula $a_n = 1.5(a_{n-1})$ with an initial value of 40 describes a sequence. Use the explicit formula to determine the 5th term of the sequence.

HABITS OF MIND

Reason What is the relationship between the explicit formula and the recursive formula? Explain. © **MP.2**

☑ Do You UNDERSTAND?

1. **? ESSENTIAL QUESTION** How are geometric sequences related to exponential functions?

2. **Vocabulary** How are *geometric sequences* similar to arithmetic sequences? How are they different?

3. **Error Analysis** For a geometric sequence with $a_1 = 3$ and a common ratio r of 1.25, Jamie writes $a_n = 1.25 \cdot (3)^{n-1}$. What mistake did Jamie make? © **MP.3**

4. **Generalize** Is a sequence geometric if each term in the sequence is x times greater than the preceding term? © **MP.8**

Do You KNOW HOW?

Determine whether the sequence is an arithmetic or a geometric sequence. If it is geometric, what is the common ratio?

5. 30, 6, 1.2, 0.24, 0.048, …

6. 0.5, 2, 8, 32, 148, …

Write the recursive formula for each geometric sequence.

7. 640, 160, 40, 10, 2.5, …

8. 2, 5, 12.5, 31.25, 78.125, …

9. What is the recursive formula for a sequence with the following explicit formula?
$a_n = 1.25 \cdot (3)^{n-1}$

10. A sequence has an initial value of 25 and a common ratio of 1.8. How can you write the sequence as a function?

 SavvasRealize.com

⊙ MODEL & DISCUSS

A radio station uses the function $f(x) = 100(3)^x$ to model the growth of Band A's fan base.

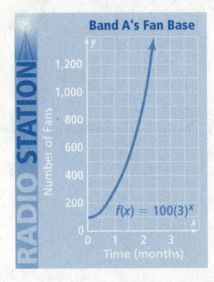

RADIO STATION

Band A's Fan Base

Number of Fans

$f(x) = 100(3)^x$

Time (months)

A. What would the graph of the function look like for Band B with a fan base growing twice as fast as Band A's fan base?

B. Compare and contrast the two graphs.

C. Look for Relationships Suppose Band C starts with a fan base of 200 fans that is growing twice as fast as Band A's fan base. Compare and contrast this new function with the previous two functions. © **MP.7**

HABITS OF MIND

Look for Relationships Is it possible for the graph of a function to have a negative value for x? Explain. © **MP.7**

EXAMPLE 1 ☑ **Try It!** **Vertical Translations of Graphs of Exponential Functions**

1. a. How does the graph of $g(x) = 2^x + 1$ compare to the graph of $f(x) = 2^x$?

b. How does the graph of $j(x) = 2^x - 1$ compare to the graph of $f(x) = 2^x$?

EXAMPLE 2 ☑ **Try It!** **Horizontal Translations of Graphs of Exponential Functions**

2. Compare the graph of each function with the graph of $f(x) = 2^x$. What effect does h have on the graph of each?

a. $g(x) = 2^{x+2}$

b. $j(x) = 2^{x-2}$

HABITS OF MIND

Use Structure Describe how the function that results in a vertical translation is different from a function that results in a horizontal translation. © **MP.7**

EXAMPLE 3   ☑ **Try It! Compare Two Different Transformations of** $f(x) = 2^x$

3. a. The graph of the function b is a vertical translation of the graph of $a(x) = 3^x$, and has a y-intercept of 0. How does the graph of $c(x) = 3^x + 1$ compare to the graph of b?

b. How does the graph of $m(x) = 3^x - 3$ compare to the graph of $p(x) = 3^x + 4$?

HABITS OF MIND

Communicate Precisely What effect does inserting a different constant into an exponential function have on the transformation of a function? Explain. ⓒ **MP.6**

☑ Do You UNDERSTAND?

1. 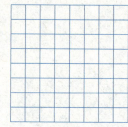 **ESSENTIAL QUESTION** How do changes in an exponential function relate to translations of its graph?

2. **Communicate Precisely** How is the effect of k on the graph of $a^x + k$ similar to the effect of h on the graph of a^{x-h}? How is it different? © MP.6

3. **Error Analysis** Tariq graphs $g(x) = 2^x + 6$ by translating the graph of $f(x) = 2^x$ six units right. What mistake did Tariq make? © MP.3

4. **Reason** As the value of k switches from a positive to a negative number, what is the effect on the graph of $f(x) = 2^{x+k}$? © MP.2

5. **Use Structure** The general form of vertical translations of exponential functions is $f(x) = a^x + k$. The general form of horizontal translations of exponential functions is $f(x) = a^{x-h}$. Why do you think one involves addition and one involves subtraction? © MP.7

Do You KNOW HOW?

Compare the graph of each function to the graph of $f(x) = 2^x$.

6. $g(x) = 2^x + 1$ 7. $p(x) = 2^{x-1}$

8. $j(x) = 2^x - 4$ 9. $g(x) = 2^{x+1}$

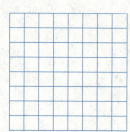   

10. Compare the function represented by the graph of $g(x) = 2^x - 3$ to the function represented by the table.

x	$h(x)$
-2	1.25
-1	1.5
0	2
1	3
2	5

Compare the graph of each function to the graph of $f(x) = 0.4^x$.

11. $g(x) = 0.4^{x+1}$ 12. $p(x) = 0.4^{x-1}$

13. $j(x) = 0.4^x + 1$ 14. $g(x) = 0.4^x - 1$

   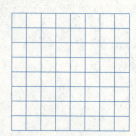

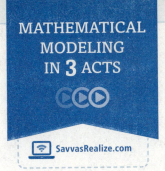

Big Time Pay Back

Most people agree that investing your money is a good idea. Some people might advise you to put money into a bank savings account. Other people might say that you should invest in the stock market. Still others think that buying bonds is the best investment option.

Is a bank savings account a good way to let your money grow? Just how much money can you make from a savings account? In the Mathematical Modeling in 3 Acts lesson, you'll see an intriguing situation about an investment option.

ACT 1 Identify the Problem

1. What is the first question that comes to mind after watching the video?

2. Write down the main question you will answer about what you saw in the video.

3. Make an initial conjecture that answers this main question.

4. Explain how you arrived at your conjecture.

5. Write a number that you know is too small.

6. Write a number that you know is too large.

7. What information will be useful to know to answer the main question? How can you get it? How will you use that information?

ACT 2 ▶ **Develop a Model**

8. Use the math that you have learned in this topic to refine your conjecture.

ACT 3 ▶ **Interpret the Results**

9. Is your refined conjecture between the highs and lows you set up earlier?

10. Did your refined conjecture match the actual answer exactly? If not, what might explain the difference?

Go Online | SavvasRealize.com

EXPLORE & REASON

Each year the Student Council conducts a food drive. At the end of the drive, the members report on the items collected.

A. Describe two different ways that the students can sort the items that were collected.

B. Model with Mathematics Write two expressions to represent the number and type of items collected. © MP.4

C. Share your expression with classmates. How are the expressions similar? How are they different? Why are they different?

HABITS OF MIND

Use Structure How does the structure of each expression relate the way you think about the items? © MP.7

☑ Assess

EXAMPLE 1 ☑ **Try It!** Understand Polynomials

1. Name each polynomial based on its degree and number of terms.

   a. $-2xy^2$

   b. $6xy - 3x + y$

EXAMPLE 2 ☑ **Try It!** Write Polynomials in Standard Form

2. Write each polynomial in standard form.

   a. $7 - 3x^3 + 6x^2$

   b. $2y - 3 - 8y^2$

EXAMPLE 3 ☑ **Try It!** Add and Subtract Monomials

3. Combine like terms and write each expression in standard form.

   a. $4x^2 - 3x - x^2 + 3x$

   b. $7y^3 - 3y + 5y^3 - 2y + 7$

HABITS OF MIND

Reason Why is it important to combine like terms and rewrite the polynomial in standard form before determining the name and number of terms of a polynomial? © **MP.2**

📶 Go Online | SavvasRealize.com

EXAMPLE 4 ✅ **Try It!** **Add Polynomials**

4. Simplify. Write each answer in standard form.

   a. $(3x^2 + 2x) + (-x + 9)$

   b. $(-2x^2 + 5x - 7) + (3x + 7)$

EXAMPLE 5 ✅ **Try It!** **Subtract Polynomials**

5. Simplify. Write each answer in standard form.

   a. $(3x^2 + 4x + 2) - (-x + 4)$

   b. $(-5x - 6) - (4x^2 + 6)$

EXAMPLE 6 ✅ **Try It!** **Apply Polynomials**

6. What expression models the difference between the total area of the large solar panels and the total area of the small solar panels?

HABITS OF MIND

Communicate Precisely A student claims that the difference of the expression $(3x^2 + 5x - 2) - (3x^2 + 5x - 2x)$ is zero. Is the student correct? Explain. Ⓒ **MP.6**

Do You UNDERSTAND?

1. ESSENTIAL QUESTION How does adding or subtracting polynomials compare to adding or subtracting integers?

2. Communicate Precisely How does the definition of the prefixes *mono-*, *bi-*, and *tri-* help when naming polynomials? **© MP.6**

3. Vocabulary Describe the relationship between the *degree of a monomial* and *the standard form a polynomial.*

4. Use Structure Explain why the sum $x + x$ is equal to $2x$ instead of x^2. **© MP.7**

5. Error Analysis Rebecca says that all monomials with the same degree are like terms. Explain Rebecca's error. **© MP.5**

Do You KNOW HOW?

Name each polynomial based on its degree and number of terms.

6. $\frac{x}{4} + 2$

7. $7x^3 + xy - 4$

Write each polynomial in standard form.

8. $2y - 3 - y^2$

9. $3x^2 - 2x + x^3 + 6$

Simplify each expression.

10. $(x^2 + 2x - 4) + (2x^2 - 5x - 3)$

11. $(3x^2 - 5x - 8) - (-4x^2 - 2x - 1)$

12. A square prism has square sides with area $x^2 + 8x + 16$ and rectangular sides with area $2x^2 + 15x + 28$. What expression represents the surface area of the square prism?

MODEL & DISCUSS

Samantha makes the abstract painting shown using vertical and horizontal lines and four colors.

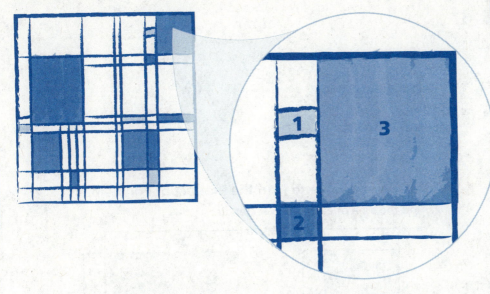

A. How can you use mathematics to describe the areas of Rectangle 1 and Rectangle 2?

B. Look for Relationships How can you use mathematics to describe the area of Rectangle 3? © MP.7

HABITS OF MIND

Communicate Precisely What information would you need to find the percentage of the painting that is red? Explain. © MP.6

Assess

EXAMPLE 1 ☑ **Try It!** **Multiply a Monomial and a Trinomial**

1. Find each product.

a. $-2x^2(x^2 + 3x + 4)$

b. $-4x(2x^2 - 3x + 5)$

EXAMPLE 2 ☑ **Try It!** **Use a Table to Find the Product of Polynomials**

2. Find the area of each green rectangle.

a.

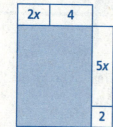

b.

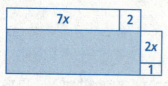

EXAMPLE 3 ☑ **Try It!** **Multiply Binomials**

3. Find each product.

a. $(5x - 4)(2x + 1)$

b. $(3x - 5)(2 + 4)$

HABITS OF MIND

Reason Could you use an area model to find the product of polynomials that have subtracted terms? Explain. Ⓒ **MP.2**

EXAMPLE 4 ☑ **Try It!** **Multiply a Trinomial and a Binomial**

    4. Find each product.

        a. $(2x - 5)(-3x^2 + 4x - 7)$

        b. $(-3x^2 + 1)(2x^2 + 3x - 4)$

EXAMPLE 5 ☑ **Try It!** **Closure and Multiplication**

    5. Why is it important that the product of two polynomials have only whole number exponents?

EXAMPLE 6 ☑ **Try It!** **Apply Multiplication of Binomials**

    6. Suppose the height of the phone in Example 6 were 1.9 times the width but all of the other conditions were the same. What expression would represent the area of the phone's surface not occupied by the screen?

HABITS OF MIND

Generalize Does closure of polynomial multiplication depend on closure of polynomial addition and subtraction? Explain. © MP.8

☑ Do You UNDERSTAND?

1. **❓ ESSENTIAL QUESTION** How does multiplying polynomials compare to multiplying integers?

2. **Use Appropriate Tools** When multiplying two variables, how is using the Distributive Property similar to using a table? Ⓒ **MP.5**

3. **Error Analysis** Mercedes states that when multiplying $4x^3(x^3 + 2x^2 - 3)$ the product is $4x^9 + 8x^6 - 12x^3$. What was Mercedes's error? Ⓒ **MP.3**

4. **Use Structure** When multiplying polynomials, why is the degree of the product different from the degree of the factors? Ⓒ **MP.7**

Do You KNOW HOW?

Find each product.

5. $-2x^3(3x^2 - 4x + 7)$

6. $(2x + 6)(x - 4)$

7. $(x - 2)(3x + 4)$

8. $(5y - 2)(4y^2 + 3y - 1)$

9. $(3x^2 + 2x - 5)(2x - 3)$

10. Find the area of the rectangle.

2x + 4

4x − 2

EXPLORE & REASON

The table gives values for x and y and different expressions.

x	y	$(x - y)(x + y)$	x^2	y^2	$(x^2 - y^2)$
7	4				
6	2				
3	9				

A. Complete the table.

B. Describe any patterns you notice.

C. Use Structure Try substituting variable expressions of the form $7p$ and $4q$ for x and y. Does the pattern still hold? Explain. © MP.7

- - - - - - - - - - - - - - - - - - - -
HABITS OF MIND

Generalize Did your exploration provide enough information establish a general rule? Explain. © MP.8

EXAMPLE 1   ☑ **Try It!** Determine the Square of a Binomial

1. Find each product.

  a. $(3x - 4)^2$

  b. 71^2

EXAMPLE 2   ☑ **Try It!** Find the Product of a Sum and a Difference

2. Find each product.

  a. $(2x - 4)(2x + 4)$

  b. $56 \cdot 44$

HABITS OF MIND

Use Appropriate Tools How do area models and algebraic expressions help you understand the patterns for the square of a binomial and for the product of a sum and a difference? © **MP.5**

 Assess

EXAMPLE 3 ☑ **Try It!** **Apply the Square of a Binomial**

3. What is the area of the square image if the area of the border is 704 square pixels and it is 4 pixels wide?

HABITS OF MIND

Communicate Precisely What mathematical terms apply in this situation? Ⓒ **MP.6**

Do You UNDERSTAND?

1. **ESSENTIAL QUESTION** What patterns are there in the product of the square of a binomial and the product of a sum and a difference?

2. **Error Analysis** Kennedy multiplies $(x - 3)(x + 3)$ and gets an answer of $x^2 - 6x - 9$. Describe and correct Kennedy's error. © **MP.3**

3. **Vocabulary** The product $(x + 6)(x - 6)$ is equivalent to an expression that is called the *difference of two squares*. Explain why the term *difference of two squares* is appropriate.

4. **Use Structure** Explain why the product of two binomials in the form $(a + b)(a - b)$ is a binomial instead of a trinomial. © **MP.7**

Do You KNOW HOW?

Write each product in standard form.

5. $(x - 7)^2$

6. $(2x + 5)^2$

7. $(x + 4)(x - 4)$

8. $(3y - 5)(3y + 5)$

Use either the square of a binomial or the difference of two squares to find the area of each rectangle.

9.

54 cm

54 cm

10.

24 in.

36 in.

MODEL & DISCUSS

A catering company has been asked to design meal boxes for entrees and side dishes.

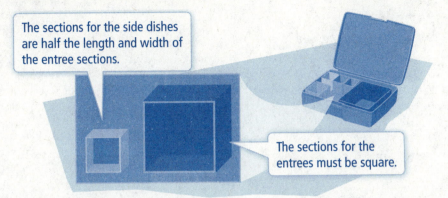

The sections for the side dishes are half the length and width of the entree sections.

The sections for the entrees must be square.

A. Design a meal box that meets each of these requirements:

  a. Equal numbers of sections for entrees and side dishes

  b. More sections for entrees than for side dishes

  c. More sections for side dishes than for entrees

B. Use Structure For each meal box from Part A, write an algebraic expression to model the area of the meal boxes. © **MP.7**

HABITS OF MIND

Construct Arguments Can you meet more than one of the three requirements with the same-sized meal box? Use a mathematical argument to support your answer.
© **MP.3**

EXAMPLE 1 ☑ **Try It!** **Find the Greatest Common Factor**

1. Find the GCF of the terms of each polynomial.

a. $15x^2 + 18$

b. $-18y^4 + 6y^3 + 24y^2$

EXAMPLE 2 ☑ **Try It!** **Factor Out the Greatest Common Factor**

2. Factor out the GCF from each polynomial.

a. $x^3 + 5x^2 - 22x$

b. $-16y^6 + 28y^4 - 20y^3$

HABITS OF MIND

Use Appropriate Tools If you model a trinomial $ax^2 + bx + c$ using algebra tiles, how can you tell if it has common factor? © **MP.5**

EXAMPLE 3   ☑ **Try It!**   **Factor a Polynomial Model**

3. Suppose the dimensions of the narrower photos were increased to 2 in. by *x* in. What expression would represent the new arrangement based on the GCF?

HABITS OF MIND

Reason If none of the terms of a polynomial have the same variable, what will be true about the GCF? ⒸMP.2

Do You UNDERSTAND?

1.  **ESSENTIAL QUESTION** How is factoring a polynomial similar to factoring integers?

2. **Look for Relationships** Why does the GCF of the variables of a polynomial have the *least* exponent of any variable term in the polynomial? © **MP.7**

3. **Reason** What is the greatest common factor of two polynomials that do not appear to have any common factors? © **MP.2**

4. **Error Analysis** Andrew factored $3x^2y - 6xy^2 + 3xy$ as $3xy(x - 2y)$. Describe and correct his error. © **MP.3**

5. **Error Analysis** Wendell says that the greatest common factor of x^6 and x^8 is x^2, since the greatest common factor of 6 and 8 is 2. Is Wendell correct? Explain. © **MP.3**

Do You KNOW HOW?

Find the GCF of each pair of monomials.

6. $10x$ and 25

7. x^3y^2 and x^5y

8. $8a^2$ and $28a^5$

9. $4x^3$ and $9y^5$

10. $12a^5b$ and $16a^4b^2$

11. $14x^{10}y^8$ and $15x^6y^9$

Factor out the GCF from each polynomial.

12. $10a^2b + 12ab^2$

13. $-3x^4 + 12x^3 - 21x^2$

14. $15x^3y - 10x^2y^3$

15. $x^{10} + x^9 - x^8$

16. $3x^3y^2 - 9xz^4 + 8y^2z$

17. $100a^7b^5 - 150a^8b^3$

EXPLORE & REASON

Consider the following puzzles.

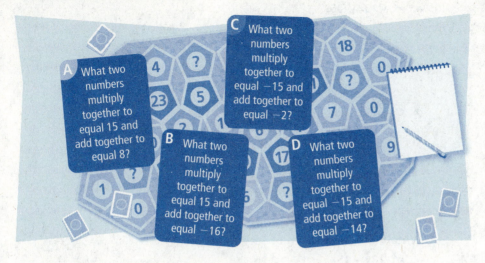

A. Find the solutions to the four puzzles shown.

B. **Look for Relationships** Write as set of four number puzzles of your own that have the same structure as these four. Describe the pattern. © **MP.7**

HABITS OF MIND

Make Sense and Persevere Can you choose any pair of integers to create a solvable puzzle? Explain. © **MP.1**

EXAMPLE 1   ☑ **Try It!**   **Understand Factoring a Trinomial**

    1. Write the factored form of each trinomial.

       a. $x^2 + 13x + 36$

       b. $x^2 + 11x + 28$

EXAMPLE 2   ☑ **Try It!**   **Factor $x^2 + bx + c$, When $b < 0$ and $c > 0$**

    2. Write the factored form of each trinomial.

       a. $x^2 - 8x + 15$

       b. $x^2 - 13x + 42$

EXAMPLE 3   ☑ **Try It!**   **Factor $x^2 + bx + c$, When $c < 0$**

    3. Write the factored form of each trinomial.

       a. $x^2 - 5x - 14$

       b. $x^2 + 6x - 16$

HABITS OF MIND

Use Structure If both *b* and *c* are negative, will the factors both be negative? Explain. ⓒ **MP.7**

EXAMPLE 4 ☑ **Try It!** Factor a Trinomial With Two Variables

4. Write the factored form of each trinomial.

   a. $x^2 + 12xy + 32y^2$

   b. $x^2 - 10xy + 21y^2$

EXAMPLE 5 ☑ **Try It!** Apply Factoring Trinomials

5. What would be the dimensions of the larger wall area you would need if you used 11 of the 1 ft-by-1 ft units while keeping the other units the same?

HABITS OF MIND

Model With Mathematics How might factoring a trinomial into a pair of binomial factors relate to a situation in a physical world? ⓒ **MP.4**

✅ Do You UNDERSTAND?

1. **ESSENTIAL QUESTION** How does recognizing patterns in the signs of the terms help you factor polynomials?

2. **Error Analysis** A student says that since $x^2 - 5x - 6$ has two negative terms, both factors of c will be negative. Explain the error the student made. Ⓒ **MP.3**

3. **Reason** What is the first step to factoring any trinomial? Explain. Ⓒ **MP.2**

4. **Communicate Precisely** To factor a trinomial $x^2 + bx + c$, why do you find the factors of c and not b? Explain. Ⓒ **MP.6**

Do You KNOW HOW?

List the factor pairs of c for each trinomial.

5. $x^2 + 17x + 16$

6. $x^2 + 4x - 21$

For each trinomial, tell whether the factor pairs of c will be both positive, both negative, or opposite signs.

7. $x^2 - 11x + 10$

8. $x^2 + 9x - 10$

9. Complete the table for factoring the trinomial $x^2 - 7x + 12$.

Factors of 12	Sum of Factors
−1 and −12	?
?	−7
−2 and −6	−8

MATHEMATICAL MODELING IN 3 ACTS

 SavvasRealize.com

Who's Right?

People often approach a problem in different ways. Sometimes their solutions are the same, but other times different approaches lead to very different, but still valid, solutions.

Suppose you had to solve a system of linear equations. You might solve it by graphing, while a classmate might use substitution. Is one way of solving a problem always better than another? Think about this during the Mathematical Modeling in 3 Acts lesson.

ACT 1 Identify the Problem

1. What is the first question that comes to mind after watching the video?

2. Write down the main question you will answer about what you saw in the video.

3. Make an initial conjecture that answers this main question.

4. Explain how you arrived at your conjecture.

5. What information will be useful to know to answer the main question? How can you get it? How will you use that information?

ACT 2 ▷ Develop a Model

6. Use the math that you have learned in the topic to refine your conjecture.

ACT 3 ▷ Interpret the Results

7. Did your refined conjecture match the actual answer exactly? If not, what might explain the difference?

EXPLORE & REASON

A website design company resizes rectangular photos so they fit on the screens of different devices.

Area: $x^2 + 7x + 12$

🛜 SavvasRealize.com

A. What expression represents the width of the photo?

B. Write three possible lengths and corresponding widths of the photo by substituting different values for x.

C. Make Sense and Persevere Why would the company use an expression to represent the area? Explain. Ⓒ **MP.1**

HABITS OF MIND

Make Sense and Persevere Can you factor all trinomials of the form $ax^2 + bx + c$ as $(px + q)(sx + t)$, when a, b, c, p, q, s, and t are integers? Explain. Ⓒ **MP.1**

EXAMPLE 1 ✅ **Try It!** **Factor Out a Common Factor**

1. Factor each trinomial.

  a. $5x^2 - 35x + 50$

  b. $6x^3 + 30x^2 + 24x$

EXAMPLE 2 ✅ **Try It!** **Understand Factoring by Grouping**

2. Factor each trinomial.

  a. $10x^2 + 17x + 3$

  b. $2x^2 + x - 21$

HABITS OF MIND

Use Appropriate Tools Why is it helpful to factor out a GCF from a trinomial before factoring it as the product of binomials? Is it essential? Explain. ©️ **MP.5**

Assess

EXAMPLE 3 ☑ **Try It!** **Factor a Trinomial Using Substitution**

3. Factor each trinomial using substitution.

a. $2x^2 - x - 6$

b. $10x^2 + 3x - 1$

HABITS OF MIND

Use Structure How does using substitution help make the process of factoring simpler? © MP.7

Do You UNDERSTAND?

1. **ESSENTIAL QUESTION** How is factoring a quadratic trinomial when $a \neq 1$ similar to factoring a quadratic trinomial when $a = 1$?

2. **Error Analysis** A student says that for $ax^2 + bx + c$ to be factorable, b must equal $a + c$. Explain the error in the student's thinking. **© MP.3**

3. **Reason** Suppose you can factor $ax^2 + bx + c$ as $(px + q)(sx + t)$, where p, q, s, and t are integers. If $c = 1$, what do you know about the two binomial factors? **© MP.2**

4. **Reason** When factoring $ax^2 + bx + c$ by substitution, why is it acceptable to multiply the polynomial by a to start? **© MP.2**

5. **Construct Arguments** Felipe is factoring the expression $2x^2 - x - 28$. He knows $-x$ should be rewritten as $7x$ plus $-8x$, but he is not sure which order to place the terms in the expression. Explain to Felipe why it does not matter what order the terms are in. **© MP.3**

Do You KNOW HOW?

List the factor pairs of ac for each trinomial.

6. $2x^2 + 7x + 4$

7. $12x^2 - 5x - 2$

Tell whether the terms of each trinomial share a common factor other than 1. If there is a common factor, identify it.

8. $15x^2 - 10x - 5$

9. $3x^3 - 2x^2 - 1$

Rewrite the *x*-term in each trinomial to factor by grouping.

10. $35x^2 + 17x + 2$

11. $12x^2 + 20x + 3$

Factor each trinomial to find possible dimensions of each rectangle.

12.

$$A = 5x^2 + 17x + 6$$

13.

$$A = 6x^2 + 7x - 5$$

Activity

7-7

Factoring Special Cases

SavvasRealize.com

CRITIQUE & EXPLAIN

Seth and Bailey are given the polynomial $8x^2 + 48x + 72$ to factor.

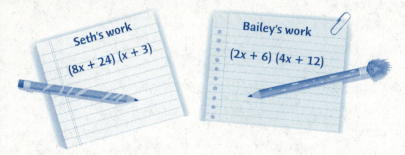

Seth's work

$(8x + 24)(x + 3)$

Bailey's work

$(2x + 6)(4x + 12)$

A. Analyze each factored expression to see if both are equivalent to the given polynomial.

B. How can the product of different pairs of expressions be equivalent?

C. **Look for Relationships** Find two other pairs of binomials that are different, but whose products are equal. © **MP.7**

HABITS OF MIND

Communicate Precisely What mathematical language was important to use in explaining the relationship between Seth's and Bailey's work? © **MP.6**

EXAMPLE 1 ☑ **Try It!** **Understand Factoring a Perfect Square**

1. Factor each trinomial.

   a. $4x^2 + 12x + 9$

   b. $x^2 - 8x + 16$

EXAMPLE 2 ☑ **Try It!** **Factor to Find a Dimension**

2. What is the radius of a cylinder that has a height of 3 in. and a volume of $\pi(27x^2 + 18x + 3)$ in.^{3}?

HABITS OF MIND

Use Structure How can you identify whether a given trinomial is a perfect square trinomial? ⒸMP.7

EXAMPLE 3   ☑ **Try It!** **Factor a Difference of Two Squares**

3. Factor each expression.

   a. $x^2 - 64$

   b. $9x^2 - 100$

EXAMPLE 4   ☑ **Try It!** **Factor Out a Common Factor**

4. Factor each expression completely.

   a. $4x^3 + 24x^2 + 36x$

   b. $50x^2 - 32y^2$

- -

HABITS OF MIND

Generalize Can you extend the difference of squares factoring pattern to $x^4 - y^4$? Explain. ⓒ **MP.8**

Do You UNDERSTAND?

1. **ESSENTIAL QUESTION** What special patterns are helpful when factoring a perfect-square trinomial and the difference of two squares?

2. Error Analysis A student says that to factor $x^2 - 4x + 2$, you should use the pattern of a difference of two squares. Explain the error in the student's thinking. © **MP.3**

3. Vocabulary How is a perfect square trinomial similar to a perfect square number? Is it possible to have a perfect square binomial? Explain.

4. Communicate Precisely How is the pattern for factoring a perfect-square trinomial like the pattern for factoring the difference of two squares? How is it different? © **MP.6**

5. Construct Arguments Why is it important to look for a common factor before factoring a trinomial? © **MP.3**

Do You KNOW HOW?

Identify the pattern you can use to factor each expression.

6. $4x^2 - 9$

7. $x^2 + 6x + 9$

8. $9x^2 - 12x + 4$

9. $5x^2 - 30x + 45$

10. $100 - 16y^2$

11. $3x^2 + 30x + 75$

Write the factored form of each expression.

12. $49x^2 - 25$

13. $36x^2 + 48x + 16$

14. $3x^3 - 12x^2 + 12x$

15. $72x^2 - 32$

16. What is the side length of the square shown below?

Area $= x^2 + 22x + 121$

EXPLORE & REASON

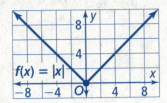

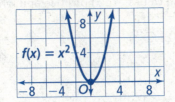

A. Look for Relationships How is the graph of $f(x) = |x|$ similar to the graph of $f(x) = x^2$? How is it different? © MP.7

B. What do you notice about the axis of symmetry in each graph?

Construct Arguments Why is the graph of $y = x^2$ always positive? © MP.3

EXAMPLE 1 ☑ **Try It!** **Identify a Quadratic Parent Function**

1. When are the values of $f(x)$ positive and when are they negative?

EXAMPLE 2 ☑ **Try It!** **Understand the Graph of** $f(x) = ax^2$

2. How does the sign of a affect the domain and range of $f(x) = ax^2$?

EXAMPLE 3 ☑ **Try It!** **Interpret Quadratic Functions from Tables**

3. A function of the form $g(x) = ax^2$ increases over the interval $x < 0$ and decreases over the interval $x > 0$. What is a possible value for a? Explain.

HABITS OF MIND

Reason Suppose you are comparing rates of change for two quadratic functions of the form $f(x) = ax^2$ over the interval $2 < x < 5$. One function has a positive rate of change and the other function has a negative rate of change over this interval. What can you conclude about the value of a in each function? Which function has a maximum value and which has a minimum value? Explain. ⓒ **MP.2**

EXAMPLE 4 ☑ **Try It!** Apply Quadratic Functions

4. By how much will the cost increase if the side length of the dance floor is increased by 2 ft?

EXAMPLE 5 ☑ **Try It!** Compare the Rate of Change

5. How do the average rates of change for $f(x) = -0.5x^2$ and $g(x) = -1.5x^2$ over the interval $-5 \leq x \leq -2$ compare?

HABITS OF MIND

Look for Relationships How does knowing whether a function of the form $f(x) = ax^2$ has a maximum or minimum value help you know over what intervals the function increases and decreases? ⒸMP.7

Do You UNDERSTAND?

1. **ESSENTIAL QUESTION** What is the quadratic parent function and how can you recognize the key features of its graph?

2. Communicate Precisely How is the graph of $f(x) = ax^2$ similar to the graph of $f(x) = x^2$? How is it different? © **MP.6**

3. Vocabulary Make a conjecture about why the term *quadratic parent function* includes the word "parent."

4. Error Analysis Abby graphed the function $f(x) = -13x^2$ by plotting the point $(-2, 52)$. Explain the error Abby made in her graph. © **MP.3**

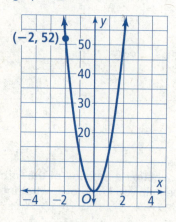

Do You KNOW HOW?

How does the value of a in each function affect its graph when compared to the graph of the quadratic parent function?

5. $g(x) = 4x^2$

6. $h(x) = 0.8x^2$

7. $j(x) = -5x^2$

8. $k(x) = -0.4x^2$

9. Given the function $f(x) = 2.5x^2 + 3$, find the average rate of change over the interval $0 \le x \le 4$. What does the average rate of change tell you about the function?

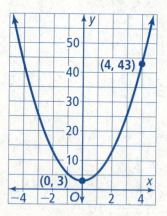

CRITIQUE & EXPLAIN

Allie states that the two graphs shown may look different, but they are actually the same figure. Esteban disagrees, stating that they are different figures because they look different.

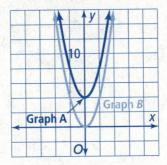

A. Give one mathematical argument to support Esteban's thinking.

B. Give one mathematical argument to support Allie's thinking.

C. Reason Who do you agree with? What argument can you give to justify your reasoning? © MP.2

HABITS OF MIND

Look for Reltionships Think about graph A and graph B and the graphs of quadratic functions. Use what you know about graphs and think of a single change that would make the graphs different. © MP.7

Try It! Understand the Graph of $g(x) = x^2 + k$

EXAMPLE 1

1. How does the graph of each function compare to the graph of $f(x) = x^2$?

a. $h(x) = x^2 + 3$

b. $j(x) = x^2 - 2$

EXAMPLE 2

 Try It! Understand the Graph of $g(x) = (x - h)^2$

2. How does the graph of each function compare to the graph of $f(x) = x^2$?

a. $h(x) = (x + 1)^2$

b. $j(x) = (x - 5)^2$

HABITS OF MIND

Make Sense and Persevere What are the values of h and k for a quadratic function with vertex (1, 2)? © **MP.8**

EXAMPLE 3

 Try It! Understand the Graph of $f(x) = a(x - h)^2 + k$

3. How does the graph of $f(x) = -3(x - 5)^2 + 7$ compare to the graph of the parent function?

EXAMPLE 4 ☑ **Try It!** **Graph Using Vertex Form**

4. Find the vertex and axis of symmetry, and sketch the graph of the function.

    a. $g(x) = -3(x - 2)^2 + 1$ **b.** $h(x) = (x + 1)^2 - 4$

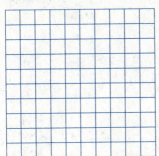 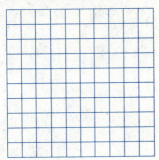

HABITS OF MIND

Construct Arguments The vertex of a parabola is in the second quadrant, and the parabola intersects the x-axis. A student says that $f(x) = -3(x + 1)^2 - 5$ could be a function for the parabola. Another student says that $f(x) = 3(x + 1)^2 + 5$ could be the function. Which student is correct? Explain. ⒸMP.3

EXAMPLE 5 ☑ **Try It!** **Use Vertex Form to Solve Problems**

5. If Deshawn does not block Chris's shot, will it be a goal? Explain.

HABITS OF MIND

Reasoning Can you always write a function in vertex form for a parabola given the coordinates of the vertex and the coordinates of another point on the parabola? Explain. ⒸMP.2

Do You UNDERSTAND?

1. **ESSENTIAL QUESTION** How can the vertex form of a quadratic function help you sketch the graph of the function?

2. Reason A table of values for the quadratic function is shown. Do the graphs of the functions g and $f(x) = 3(x - 1)^2 + 2$ have the same axis of symmetry? Explain. **© MP.2**

x	g(x)
−4	8
−2	3
0	0
6	3

3. Use Structure How are the form and the graph of $f(x) = (x - h)^2 + k$ similar to the form and graph of $f(x) = |x - h| + k$? How are they different? **© MP.7**

4. Error Analysis Sarah said the vertex of the function $f(x) = (x + 2)^2 + 6$ is (2, 6). Is she correct? Explain your answer. **© MP.3**

Do You KNOW HOW?

Graph each function.

5. $g(x) = x^2 + 5$

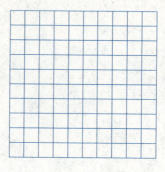

6. $f(x) = (x - 2)^2$

7. $h(x) = -2(x + 4)^2 + 1$

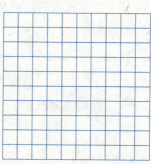

8. Write a function in vertex form for the parabola shown below.

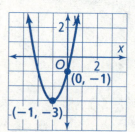

9. The height of a ball thrown into the air is a quadratic function of time. The ball is thrown from a height of 6 ft above the ground. After 1 second, the ball reaches its maximum height of 22 ft above the ground. Write the equation of the function in vertex form.

EXPLORE & REASON

Three functions of the form $f(x) = ax^2 + bx$ are graphed for $a = 2$ and different values of b.

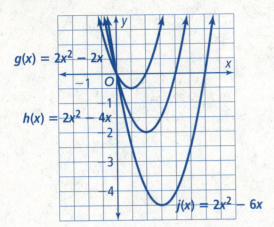

$g(x) = 2x^2 - 2x$

$h(x) = 2x^2 - 4x$

$j(x) = 2x^2 - 6x$

A. What do the graphs have in common? In what ways do they differ?

B. What do you notice about the *x*-intercepts of each graph? What do you notice about the *y*-intercepts of each graph?

C. Look for Relationships Look at the ratio $\frac{b}{a}$ for each function and compare it to its graph. What do you notice? © MP.7

- -

HABITS OF MIND

Construct Arguments Can more than one parabola have the same description? Explain. © MP.3

EXAMPLE 1 ☑ **Try It!** **Analyze the Axis of Symmetry for** $f(x) = ax^2 + bx + c$

1. Evaluate $f(x) = ax^2 + bx + c$ for $x = 0$. How does $f(0)$ relate to result in Example 1?

EXAMPLE 2 ☑ **Try It!** **Graph a Quadratic Function in Standard Form**

2. Graph each function. What are the y-intercept, the axis of symmetry, and the vertex of each function?

   a. $f(x) = x^2 + 2x + 4$

   b. $g(x) = -0.75x^2 + 3x - 4$

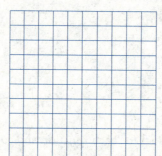   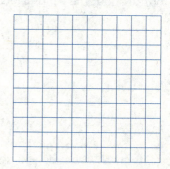

HABITS OF MIND

Use Appropriate Tools Suppose you want to graph a quadratic function in standard form on a graphing calculator. How could finding the vertex, axis of symmetry, and y-intercept of the function help you choose a viewing window for the graph? © **MP.5**

EXAMPLE 3 **Try It!** Compare Properties of Quadratic Functions

3. Compare $f(x) = -0.3x^2 - 0.6x - 0.2$ to function g, shown in the graph. What are the maximum values? Which function has the greater maximum value?

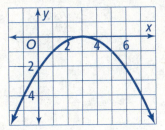

HABITS OF MIND

Reason In Example 3, how can you tell from the equation of function f that the function has a maximum? How can you tell from the table that the function representing Fountain B has a maximum? © **MP.2**

EXAMPLE 4 **Try It!** Analyze the Structure of Different Forms

4. Suppose the path of the ball in Example 4 is $f(x) = -0.25(x - 1)^2 + 6.25$. Find the ball's initial and maximum heights.

HABITS OF MIND

Use Structure Consider the different forms of the quadratic function. Which form would you use to find the y-intercept of its graph? Which form would you use to find the maximum or minimum of the function? Explain. © **MP.7**

Do You UNDERSTAND?

1. **ESSENTIAL QUESTION** How is the standard form of a quadratic function different from the vertex form?

2. **Communicate Precisely** How are the form and graph of $f(x) = ax^2 + bx + c$ similar to the form and graph of $g(x) = ax^2 + bx$? How are they different? **MP.6**

3. **Vocabulary** How can you write a function in standard form, given its vertex form?

4. **Error Analysis** Sage began graphing $f(x) = -2x^2 + 4x + 9$ by finding the axis of symmetry $x = -1$. Explain the error Sage made. **MP.3**

Do You KNOW HOW?

Graph each function. For each, identify the axis of symmetry, the y-intercept, and the coordinates of the vertex.

5. $f(x) = 2x^2 + 8x - 1$

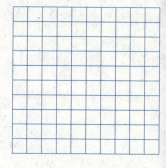

6. $f(x) = -0.5x^2 + 2x + 3$

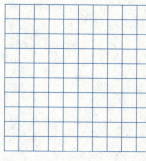

7. $f(x) = -3x^2 - 6x - 5$

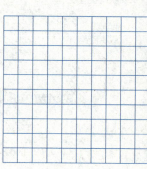

8. $f(x) = 0.25x^2 - 0.5x - 6$

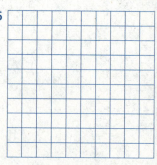

9. A water balloon is tossed into the air. The function $h(x) = -0.5(x - 4)^2 + 9$ gives the height, in feet, of the balloon from the surface of a pool as a function of the balloon's horizontal distance from where it was first tossed. Will the balloon hit the ceiling 12 ft above the pool? Explain.

MODEL & DISCUSS

The graphic shows the heights of a supply package dropped from a helicopter hovering above ground.

Time	Height
0 s	350 ft
1 s	335 ft
2 s	283 ft
3 s	206 ft
4 s	96 ft
Ground	

A. Model With Mathematics Would a linear function be a good model for the data? Explain. © MP.4

B. Would a quadratic function be a good model for the data? Explain.

HABITS OF MIND

Reason Compare the rate of change for the function representing the supply-package heights for the interval from 0 to 1 second and for the interval from 3 to 4 seconds. What do these rates of change represent, and what do they reveal about how quickly the supply package is falling over time? © MP.2

EXAMPLE 1 ☑ **Try It!** Use Quadratic Functions to Model Area

1. Suppose the length of the pool in Example 1 is 3 times the area of the width. How does the function that represents the combined area of the pool and deck change? Explain.

EXAMPLE 2 ☑ **Try It!** Model Vertical Motion

2. Find the diver's maximum height above the water if he dives from a 20-ft platform with an initial velocity of 8 ft/s.

HABITS OF MIND

Communicate Precisely In Example 2, what units are used for the initial height and velocity? How do these units relate to the coefficient of the t^2-term? Suppose the problem expressed the initial height and velocity using meters. What value would be used for the coefficient of the t^2-term? Ⓒ **MP.6**

EXAMPLE 3 ☑ **Try It! Assess the Fit of a Function by Analyzing Residuals**

3. Make a scatterplot of the data and graph the function
$f(x) = -8x^2 + 95x + 745$. Make a residual plot and describe how well
the function fits the data.

Price Increase ($)	0	1	2	3	4
Sales ($)	730	850	930	951	1010

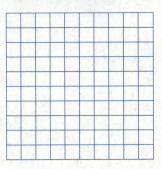

EXAMPLE 4 ☑ **Try It! Fit a Quadratic Function to Data**

4. Use the model in Example 4 to determine the predicted revenue after the
6th and 7th price increases. What do you notice?

- - - - - - - - - - - - - -
HABITS OF MIND

Construct Arguments A student thinks that the first list on the graphing
calculator screen shown in Step 1 of Example 4 should show the admission
prices in dollars: 5, 6, 7, 8, and 9. Explain why these prices are not used for
this list. Ⓒ **MP.3**

Do You UNDERSTAND?

1. **ESSENTIAL QUESTION** What kinds of real-world situations can be modeled by quadratic functions?

2. **Look for Relationships** How is the function $h(t) = -16t^2 + bt + c$ related to vertical motion? © **MP.7**

3. **Vocabulary** What does it mean in a real-world situation when the *initial velocity* is 0?

4. **Error Analysis** Chen uses $h(t) = -16t^2 + 6t + 16$ to determine the height of a ball t seconds after it is thrown at an initial velocity of 16 ft/s from an initial height of 6 ft. Describe the error Chen made. © **MP.3**

Do You KNOW HOW?

Write a vertical motion model in the form $h(t) = -16t^2 + v_0t + h_0$ for each situation presented. For each situation, determine how long, in seconds, it takes the thrown object to reach maximum height.

5. Initial velocity: 32 ft/s; initial height: 20 ft

6. Initial velocity: 120 ft/s; initial height: 50 ft

7. A rectangular patio has a length four times its width. It also has a 3-ft wide brick border around it. Write a quadratic function to determine the area of the patio and border?

8. The data are modeled by $f(x) = -2x^2 + 16.3x + 40.7$. What does the graph of the residuals tell you about the fit of the model?

x	y
1	55.0
2	65.3
3	71.6
4	73.9
5	72.2

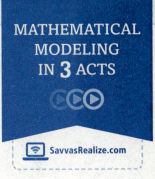
▶ The Long Shot

Have you ever been to a basketball game where they hold contests at halftime? A popular contest is one where the contestant needs to make a basket from half court to win a prize. Contestants often shoot the ball in different ways. They might take a regular basketball shot, a hook shot, or an underhand toss.

What's the best way to shoot the basketball to make a basket? Think about this during this Mathematical Modeling in 3 Acts lesson.

ACT 1 ▶ Identify the Problem

1. What is the first question that comes to mind after watching the video?

2. Write down the Main Question you will answer.

3. Make an initial conjecture that answers this Main Question.

4. Explain how you arrived at your conjecture.

ACT 2 ▷ Develop a Model

5. Use the math that you have learned in the topic to refine your conjecture.

ACT 3 ▷ Interpret the Results

6. Did your refined conjecture match the actual answer exactly? If not, what might explain the difference?

8-5

Linear,
Exponential,
and
Quadratic
Models

SavvasRealize.com

MODEL & DISCUSS

Jacy and Emma use different functions to model the value of a bike x years after it is purchased. Each function models the data in the table.

Jacy's function: $f(x) = -14.20x + 500$

Emma's function: $f(x) = 500(0.85)^x$

Time (yr)	Value ($)
0	500.00
1	485.20
2	472.13
3	461.00
4	452.10

A. **Make Sense and Persevere** Why did Jacy and Emma not choose a quadratic function to model the data? © **MP.1**

B. Whose function do you think is a better model? Explain.

C. Do you agree with this statement? Explain why or why not.

   To ensure that you are finding the best model for a table of data, you need to find the values of the functions for the same values of x.

HABITS OF MIND

Communicate Precisely How is finding the best model for data in a real-world situation similar to finding the best model in a mathematical situation? How is it different? © **MP.6**

EXAMPLE 1 ☑ **Try It!** **Determine Which Function Type Represents Data**

1. Does a linear, quadratic, or exponential function best model the data? Explain.

a.

x	0	1	2	3	4
y	−2	−5	−14	−29	−50

b.

x	−2	−1	0	1	2
y	4	12	36	108	324

EXAMPLE 2 ☑ **Try It!** **Choose a Function Type for Real-World Data**

2. Determine whether a linear, quadratic, or exponential function best models the data. Then, use regression to find the function that models the data.

x	0	1	2	3	4
y	100	89.5	78.9	68.4	57.8

HABITS OF MIND

Reason If a table of data does not have common differences or a common ratio, can you still make predictions about other data points in the data set? Explain. ⓒ MP.2

EXAMPLE 3 ☑ **Try It!** **Compare Linear, Exponential, and Quadratic Growth**

3. Compare the functions $f(x) = 3x + 2$, $g(x) = 2x^2 + 3$, and $h(x) = 2^x$. Show that as x increases, $h(x)$ will eventually exceed $f(x)$ and $g(x)$.

HABITS OF MIND

Generalize How can the rate of change help determine the type of function that best fits the data? © **MP.8**

Do You UNDERSTAND?

1. ESSENTIAL QUESTION How can you determine whether a linear, exponential, or quadratic function best models data?

2. Reason The growth of a function is less from $x = 1$ to $x = 4$ than from $x = 5$ to $x = 8$. What type of function could it be? Explain. © MP.2

3. Error Analysis Kiyo used a quadratic function to model data with constant first differences. Explain the error Kiyo made. © MP.3

Do You KNOW HOW?

Determine whether the data are best modeled by a linear, quadratic, or exponential function.

4.

x	0	1	2	3	4
y	−2	1	10	25	46

5.

x	−2	−1	0	1	2
y	2	7	12	17	22

6. A company's profit from a certain product is represented by $P(x) = -5x^2 + 1{,}125x - 5{,}000$, where x is the price of the product. Compare the growth in profits from $x = 120$ to $x = 140$ and from $x = 140$ to $x = 160$. What do you notice?

Activity

9-1

Solving Quadratic Equations Using Graphs and Tables

SavvasRealize.com

EXPLORE & REASON

The path of a golf ball hit from the ground resembles the shape of a parabola.

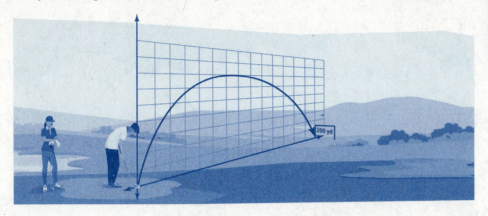

200 yd

A. What point represents the golf ball before it is hit off the ground?

B. What point represents the golf ball when it lands on the ground?

C. **Look for Relationships** Explain how the points in Part A and B are related to the ball's distance from the ground. © **MP.7**

- -

HABITS OF MIND

Communicate Precisely In a table, how are independent variables different from dependent variables? Explain. © **MP.6**

EXAMPLE 1 ☑ **Try It!** Recognize Solutions of Quadratic Equations

1. What are the solutions of each equation?

    a. $x^2 - 36 = 0$

    b. $x^2 + 6x + 9 = 0$

EXAMPLE 2 ☑ **Try It!** Solve Quadratic Equations Using Tables

2. Find the solutions for $4x^2 + 3x - 7 = 0$ using a table. If approximating, give the answer to the nearest tenth.

HABITS OF MIND

Communicate Precisely When is it easier to solve a quadratic equation by graphing? When is it easier to solve a quadratic equation using a table? Justify you answers. Ⓒ **MP.6**

 Assess

EXAMPLE 3   ☑ **Try It!** Use Approximate Solutions

3. At the next tee, a golf ball was hit and modeled by $-16x^2 + 11x + 6 = 0$. When will the golf ball hit the ground?

HABITS OF MIND

Look for Relationships How is the graph of an absolute value function related to the graph of a quadratic function? Explain. ⓒ **MP.7**

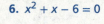

Do You UNDERSTAND?

1. **ESSENTIAL QUESTION** How can graphs and tables help you solve quadratic equations?

2. **Reason** In a table that shows no exact solutions, how do you know if there are any solutions? How can you find an approximate solution? © **MP.2**

3. **Error Analysis** Eli says that the solutions to $x^2 + 100 = 0$ are -10 and 10 because 10^2 is 100. What is the error that Eli made? © **MP.3**

4. **Communicate Precisely** When you graph a quadratic function, the y-intercept appears to be 1, and the x-intercepts appear to be -4 and 2.5. Which values represent the solution(s) to the related quadratic equation of the function? How can you verify this? Explain. © **MP.6**

Do You KNOW HOW?

Use each graph to find the solution of the equation.

5. $-x^2 + 2x - 1 = 0$ 6. $x^2 + x - 6 = 0$

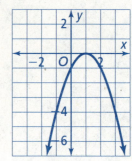 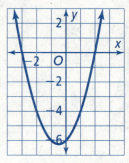

Solve each quadratic equation by graphing the related function.

7. $x^2 - 2x - 3 = 0$ 8. $x^2 + x + 1 = 0$

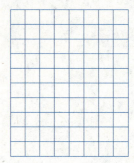 

Find the solutions of each equation using a table. Round approximate solutions to the nearest tenth.

9. $x^2 + 3x - 4 = 0$

10. $3x^2 - 2x + 1 = 0$

11. What are the solutions of $-5x^2 + 10x + 2 = 0$? Round approximate solutions to the nearest tenth.

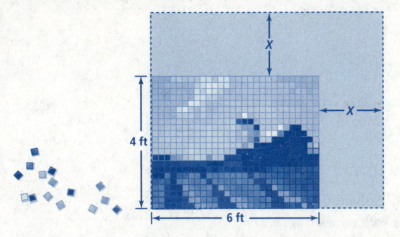

MODEL & DISCUSS

An artist has started a mosaic tile design on a wall. She needs to cover the entire wall.

A. Write expressions to represent the length of the wall and width of the wall.

B. Use Structure What expression represents the area of the entire wall? Explain. © **MP.7**

C. How can you determine the area of the part of the wall that the artist has not yet covered?

- -

HABITS OF MIND

Make Sense and Persevere How might factoring help you solve a quadratic equation? Explain. © **MP.1**

EXAMPLE 1 ✓ **Try It!** **Use the Zero-Product Property**

1. Solve each equation.

   a. $(2x - 1)(x + 3) = 0$

   b. $(2x + 3)(3x - 1) = 0$

EXAMPLE 2 ✓ **Try It!** **Solve by Factoring**

2. Solve each equation by factoring.

   a. $x^2 + 16x + 64 = 0$

   b. $x^2 - 12x = 64$

EXAMPLE 3 ✓ **Try It!** **Use Factoring to Solve a Real-World Problem**

3. A picture inside a frame has an area of 375 cm². What is the width of the frame?

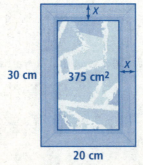

30 cm   375 cm² x x

20 cm

- -

HABITS OF MIND

Reason Why is there only one solution to a quadratic equation in the form $x^2 + 2ax + a^2 = 0$? © **MP.2**

EXAMPLE 4   ✅ **Try It!** **Use Factored Form to Graph a Quadratic Function**

4. Use factoring to graph the function $f(x) = 2x^2 + 5x - 3$.

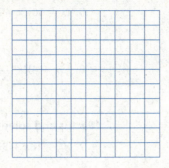

EXAMPLE 5   ✅ **Try It!** **Write the Factored Form of a Quadratic Function**

5. What is the factored form of the function?

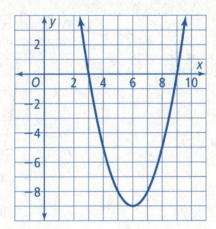

HABITS OF MIND

Communicate Precisely How do the factors of a function relate to the graph of the function? Explain. Ⓒ **MP.6**

Do You UNDERSTAND?

1. **ESSENTIAL QUESTION** How does factoring help you solve quadratic equations?

2. **Use Structure** Compare the solutions of $2x^2 + 5x - 7 = 0$ and $4x^2 + 10x - 14 = 0$. What do you notice? Explain. © **MP.7**

3. **Vocabulary** What is the *Zero-Product Property*? When can you use it to solve a quadratic equation? Explain.

4. **Generalize** If a perfect-square trinomial has a value of 0, how many solutions does the equation have? Explain. © **MP.8**

Do You KNOW HOW?

Solve each equation.

5. $(x - 10)(x + 20) = 0$

6. $(3x + 4)(x - 4) = 0$

Factor and solve each equation.

7. $x^2 + 18x + 32 = 0$

8. $x^2 - 4x - 21 = 0$

Solve each equation.

9. $x^2 + 2x = -1$

10. $x^2 - 8x = 9$

11. $2x^2 + x = 15$

12. $5x^2 - 19x = -18$

13. Write a quadratic equation, in factored form, whose solutions correspond to the *x*-intercepts of the quadratic function shown below.

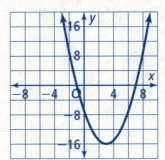

14. Factor the equation $x^2 - 6x + 5 = 0$. Find the coordinates of the vertex of the related function and graph the equation $x^2 - 6x + 5$.

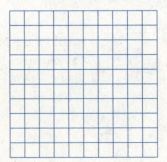

 SavvasRealize.com

⏱ EXPLORE & REASON

The table shows the relationship between the area of a square, the side length of the square, and the square root of the area. A square with an area of 4 and a side length of 2 is shown at the right.

Area of Square (square units)	Area $= s^2$	Side Length, s (units)
1	$1 = \sqrt{s}$	1
4	$4 = \sqrt{s}$	2
9	$9 = \sqrt{s}$	3
16	$16 = \sqrt{s}$	4
25	$25 = \sqrt{s}$	5

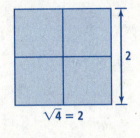

$\sqrt{4} = 2$

A. What is the side length of a square with an area of 49 square units?

B. Use Structure Between what two consecutive integers is $\sqrt{20}$? How do you know? © MP.7

C. Think of three squares that have a side length between 3 and 4. What is the area of each square?

- -

HABITS OF MIND

Communicate Precisely Is the $\sqrt{90}$ closer to 9 or 10? Explain how you know. © MP.6

EXAMPLE 1 ✅ **Try It!** **Use Properties to Rewrite Radical Expressions**

1. Compare each pair of radical expressions.

a. $\sqrt{36}$ and $3\sqrt{6}$

b. $6\sqrt{2}$ and $\sqrt{72}$

EXAMPLE 2 ✅ **Try It!** **Write Equivalent Radical Expressions**

2. Rewrite each expression to remove perfect square factors other than 1 in the radicand.

a. $\sqrt{44}$

b. $3\sqrt{27}$

EXAMPLE 3 ✅ **Try It!** **Write Equivalent Radical Expressions With Variables**

3. Rewrite each expression to remove perfect square factors other than 1 in the radicand.

a. $\sqrt{25x^3}$

b. $5\sqrt{4x^{17}}$

HABITS OF MIND

Generalize How does the exponent of a variable help you to determine if the term is a perfect square? © **MP.8**

EXAMPLE 4   ☑ **Try It!** **Multiply Radical Expressions**

4. Write an expression for each product without perfect square factors in the radicand.

   a. $\frac{1}{2}\sqrt{21x^3} \cdot 4\sqrt{7x^2}$

   b. $2\sqrt{12x^9} \cdot \sqrt{18x^5}$

EXAMPLE 5   ☑ **Try It!** **Write a Radical Expression**

5. Another cone has a slant height s that is 5 times the radius. What is the simplified expression for the height in terms of the radius?

HABITS OF MIND

Reason When is a radical expression in simplest form? Justify your answer. ⓒ **MP.2**

Do You UNDERSTAND?

1. **ESSENTIAL QUESTION** How does rewriting radicals in different forms help you communicate your answer?

2. **Vocabulary** State the *Product Property of Square Roots* in your own words.

3. **Communicate Precisely** Write an expression for $\sqrt{32}$ without any perfect square factors in the radicand. Explain your steps. **MP.6**

4. **Error Analysis** Rikki says that the product $\sqrt{3x^3} \cdot \sqrt{x}$ is $3x^2$. Explain Rikki's error and write the correct product. **MP.3**

5. **Construct Arguments** Is $\sqrt{45}$ in simplest form? Explain. **MP.3**

6. **Make Sense and Persevere** Describe how you would simplify an expression so that there are no perfect square factors in the radicand. **MP.1**

Do You KNOW HOW?

Factor each radicand using the Product Property of Square Roots.

7. $\sqrt{80}$

8. $\sqrt{x^7}$

9. $\sqrt{40x^4}$

10. $\sqrt{11x^5}$

11. $\sqrt{200}$

12. $8\sqrt{8}$

Write an expression for each product without a perfect square factor other than 1 in the radicand.

13. $4\sqrt{3x^3} \cdot 3\sqrt{2x^2}$

14. $x\sqrt{2x^5} \cdot 2x\sqrt{8x}$

15. $\sqrt{7x} \cdot 3\sqrt{10x^7}$

Compare each pair of radical expressions by writing each expression as a product of square roots in simplest form.

16. $\sqrt{72}$ and $2\sqrt{50}$

17. $5\sqrt{28}$ and $\sqrt{119}$

Write each expression so there are no perfect square factors other than 1 in the radicand.

18. $\sqrt{100x^8}$

19. $4x^2y\sqrt{2x^4y^6}$

EXPLORE & REASON

A developer is building 3 recreation square areas on a parcel of land. He has not decided what to do with the enclosed triangular area in the center.

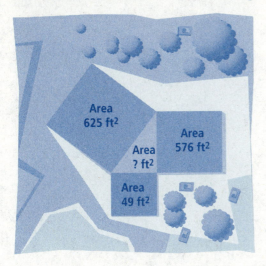

Area 625 ft²

Area 576 ft²

Area ? ft²

Area 49 ft²

A. How can you determine the side lengths of the triangle in the center?

B. What relationships do you notice among the areas of the squares?

C. Look for Relationships How can the developer adjust this plan so that each recreation area covers less area but still has a similar triangular section in the middle? Explain. Ⓒ **MP.7**

HABITS OF MIND

Make Sense and Persevere The Product Property of Square Roots states that $\sqrt{ab} = \sqrt{a} \cdot \sqrt{b}$ when both a and b are greater than or equal to 0. Explain why it is essential that a and b are greater than or equal to 0. Ⓒ **MP.1**

EXAMPLE 1   ☑ **Try It!** **Solve Equations of the Form** $x^2 = a$

1. Solve each equation by inspection.

   a. $x^2 = 169$

   b. $x^2 = -16$

EXAMPLE 2   ☑ **Try It!** **Solve Equations of the Form** $ax^2 = c$

2. What are the solutions for each equation? If the solution is not a perfect square, state what two integers the solution is between.

   a. $5x^2 = 125$

   b. $-\frac{1}{2}x^2 = -36$

HABITS OF MIND

Construct Arguments What is an advantage of solving a quadratic equation using square roots? What is a disadvantage? Explain your reasoning. ©️ **MP.3**

EXAMPLE 3 ☑ **Try It!** Solve Equations of the Form $ax^2 + b = c$

    3. Solve the quadratic equations.

      a. $-5x^2 - 19 = 144$

      b. $3x^2 + 17 = 209$

EXAMPLE 4 ☑ **Try It!** Determine a Reasonable Solution

    4. Find the distance from the base of the tower to the midpoint of the guy-wire.

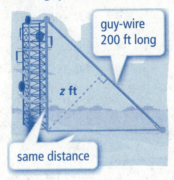

guy-wire 200 ft long

z ft

same distance

HABITS OF MIND

Communicate Precisely When is the negative square root not a reasonable solution? Explain and give an example. Ⓒ **MP.6**

Do You UNDERSTAND?

1. **ESSENTIAL QUESTION** How can square roots be used to solve quadratic equations?

2. **Construct Arguments** How many solutions does $ax^2 = c$ have if a and c have different signs? Explain. **© MP.3**

3. **Reason** How do you decide when to use the $\pm$ symbol when solving a quadratic equation? **© MP.2**

4. **Error Analysis** Trey solved $2x^2 = 98$ and said that the solution in 7. Is he correct? Why or why not? **© MP.3**

5. **Communicate Precisely** How is solving an equation in the form $ax^2 = c$ similar to solving an equation in the form $ax^2 + b = c$? How are they different?

Do You KNOW HOW?

Solve each equation by inspection.

6. $x^2 = 400$

7. $x^2 = -25$

Solve each equation.

8. $3x^2 = 400$

9. $-15x^2 = -90$

10. $2x^2 + 7 = 31$

11. $2x^2 - 7 = 38$

12. $-4x^2 - 1 = 48$

13. $-4x^2 + 50 = 1$

14. $3x^2 + 2x^2 = 150$

15. $3x^2 + 18 = 5x^2$

Solve for x.

16.
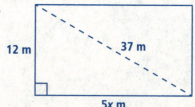
12 m, 37 m, 5x m

17.
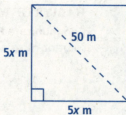
5x m, 50 m, 5x m

CRITIQUE AND EXPLAIN

Enrique and Nadeem used different methods to solve the equation $x^2 - 6x + 9 = 16$.

Enrique

$x^2 - 6x + 9 = 16$

$x^2 - 6x - 7 = 0$

$(x - 7)(x + 1) = 0$

$x - 7 = 0$ OR $x + 1 = 0$

$x = 7$ OR $x = -1$

The solutions are 7 and –1.

Nadeem

$x^2 - 6x + 9 = 16$

$(x - 3)^2 = 16$

$x - 3 = \pm 4$

$x - 3 = 4$ OR $x - 3 = -4$

$x = 7$ OR $x = -1$

The solutions are 7 and –1.

A. Critique Enrique's work. If his method is valid, explain the reasoning he used. If his method is not valid, explain why not.

B. Critique Nadeem's work. If his method is valid, explain the reasoning he used. If his method is not valid, explain why not.

C. Use Structure Can you use either Enrique's or Nadeem's method to solve the equation $x^2 + 10x + 25 = 3$? Explain. Ⓒ **MP.7**

HABITS OF MIND

Reason Explain how the Properties of Equality are used to solve equations. Ⓒ **MP.2**

EXAMPLE 1 ☑ **Try It!** **Complete the Square**

1. What value of c completes the square?

   a. $x^2 + 12x + c$

   b. $x^2 + 8x + c$

EXAMPLE 2 ☑ **Try It!** **Solve $x^2 + bx + c = 0$**

2. What are the solutions of each quadratic equation? Solve by completing the square.

   a. $x^2 + 10x - 9 = 0$

   b. $x^2 - 8x - 6 = 0$

EXAMPLE 3 ☑ **Try It!** **Complete the Square When $a \neq 1$ Initially**

3. A maze and walkway with the same total area of 5,616 square yards has a walkway that is one yard wide. What are the dimensions of this maze?

HABITS OF MIND

Reason Is it possible for the value used to complete the square to be negative? Explain. ⓒ **MP.2**

EXAMPLE 4 ☑ **Try It!** **Use Completing the Square to Write a Quadratic Function In Vertex Form**

4. What is the vertex form of each function?

a. $y = x^2 - 2x + 3$

b. $y = x^2 + 6x + 25$

EXAMPLE 5 ☑ **Try It!** **Write Vertex Form When $a \neq 1$**

5. Find the minimum value of the function $y = 7x^2 + 168x + 105$.

HABITS OF MIND

Communicate Precisely How is completing the square related to writing the vertex form of a function? Explain. ⓒ **MP.6**

Do You UNDERSTAND?

1. **ESSENTIAL QUESTION** How is the technique of completing the square helpful for analyzing quadratic functions?

2. **Vocabulary** Why does it make sense to describe adding 25 to $x^2 + 10x$ as *completing the square*?

3. **Error Analysis** A student began solving $x^2 + 8x = 5$ by writing $x^2 + 8x + 16 = 5$. Explain the error the student made. **© MP.3**

4. **Communicate Precisely** How is changing a quadratic function from standard form to vertex form like solving a quadratic equation by completing the square? How is it different? **© MP.6**

5. **Look for Relationships** Why is it necessary for the coefficient of x^2 to be 1 before completing the square? **© MP.7**

Do You KNOW HOW?

Find the value of c that makes each expression a perfect-square trinomial.

6. $x^2 + 26x + c$

7. $x^2 + 2x + c$

8. $x^2 + 18x + c$

Solve each equation.

9. $x^2 + 8x = -1$

10. $2x^2 - 24x - 4 = 0$

11. $x^2 - 4x = 7$

Write each function in vertex form.

12. $y = x^2 + 4x - 5$

13. $y = 5x^2 - 10x + 7$

14. $y = x^2 + 8x - 15$

EXPLORE & REASON

Three quadratic equations are shown on the whiteboard.

$$x^2 - 6x + 12 = 0$$
$$x^2 - 6x + 9 = 0$$
$$x^2 - 6x - 5 = 0$$

A. How many real solutions are there for each of the quadratic equations shown? Explain your answer.

B. Use Appropriate Tools Use your graphing calculator to graph the related function for each equation. What are the function equations for each graph's reflection over the *x*-axis? Explain how you found the function equations.
Ⓒ **MP.5**

C. What do you notice about the graphs that have zero *x*-intercepts? One *x*-intercept? Two *x*-intercepts?

HABITS OF MIND

Reason How can the number of solutions to a quadratic equation be determined by inspecting its graph? Ⓒ **MP.2**

EXAMPLE 1 ☑ **Try It!** **Derive the Quadratic Formula**

1. What is the maximum number of solutions the quadratic formula can give? Explain

EXAMPLE 2 ☑ **Try It!** **Use the Quadratic Formula**

2. Find the solutions of each equation using the quadratic formula.

   a. $21 - 4x = x^2$

   b. $x^2 - 2x = 24$

HABITS OF MIND

Look for Relationships Using the quadratic formula, how can you tell when a quadratic equation has only one solution? ⒸMP.7

EXAMPLE 3   ☑ **Try It!** **Find Approximate Solutions**

3. The height of another frog over time is modeled by the function $y = -16t^2 + 10t + 0.3$. How many seconds is this frog in the air before landing on the ground? Round your answer to the nearest hundredth.

EXAMPLE 4   ☑ **Try It!** **Understand and Use the Discriminant**

4. Use the discriminant to find the number of roots of each equation.

   a. $x^2 - 10x + 25 = 0$

   b. $-x^2 - 6x - 10 = 0$

HABITS OF MIND

Reason If the equation $4x^2 - bx + 9 = 0$ has only 1 solution, what is the value of b? ⓒ **MP.2**

Do You UNDERSTAND?

1. ESSENTIAL QUESTION When should you use the quadratic formula to solve equations?

2. Reason What value of b^2 is needed for there to be exactly one real solution of a quadratic equation? Explain. © **MP.2**

3. Vocabulary How are the *roots* of a quadratic equation related to its *discriminant*?

4. Error Analysis A student says that the quadratic formula cannot be used to solve $-23x^2 + 5 = 0$. Explain the error the student made. © **MP.3**

5. Reason When is completing the square better than using the quadratic formula? © **MP.2**

Do You KNOW HOW?

Identify *a*, *b*, and *c* in each of the quadratic equations.

6. $4x^2 + 2x - 1 = 0$

7. $-x^2 + 31x + 7 = 0$

8. $2x^2 - 10x - 3 = 0$

9. $x^2 + x - 1 = 0$

Given the discriminant of a quadratic equation, determine the number of real solutions.

10. 8

11. −3

12. 0

13. 1

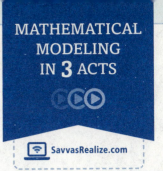

Unwrapping Change

When you arrange a group of objects in different ways, it seems like the space they take up has changed. But, the number of objects didn't change!

We use coin wrappers to store coins in an efficient way. How much more efficient is it than the alternative? Think about this during the Mathematical Modeling in 3 Acts lesson.

ACT 1 Identify the Problem

1. What is the first question that comes to mind after watching the video?

2. Write down the main question you will answer about what you saw in the video.

3. Make an initial conjecture that answers this main question.

4. Explain how you arrived at your conjecture.

5. What information will be useful to know to answer the main question? How can you get it? How will you use that information?

ACT 2 ▸ Develop a Model

6. Use the math that you have learned in this Topic to refine your conjecture.

ACT 3 ▸ Interpret the Results

7. Did your refined conjecture match the actual answer exactly? If not, what might explain the difference?

⏻ MODEL & DISCUSS

An architect is designing an archway for a building that has a 9 ft ceiling. She is
working with the constraints shown.

7 ft

5 ft

A. Find a quadratic model for the arches if the highest point of the arch touches
the ceiling.

B. Use Structure Describe how to change the model so that the highest point of
the arch does not touch the ceiling. © MP.7

HABITS OF MIND

Look for Relationships How is finding the model above like solving a system of linear
equations? How is it different. © MP.5

EXAMPLE 1   ☑ **Try It!** **Understand Linear-Quadratic Systems of Equations**

1. How many solutions does the system of equations at the right have? Explain.

$y = x$
$y = x^2$

EXAMPLE 2   ☑ **Try It!** **Solve a Linear-Quadratic Equation by Graphing**

2. What are the solutions of each of the equations? Rewrite each as a system of equations and graph to solve.

a. $x^2 + 1 = x + 3$

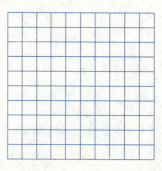

b. $5 - 0.5x^2 = -0.5x + 2$

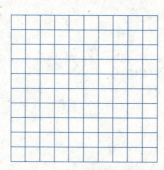

- -
HABITS OF MIND

Communicate Precisely How could you use a table to solve a system of linear and quadratic equations? When does it make sense to use this method? Explain. ⓒ **MP.6**

EXAMPLE 3   ☑ **Try It!** **Solve Systems of Equations Using Elimination**

3. Use elimination to solve each system of equations.

a. $y = -x + 4$
   $y = x^2 - 2$

b. $y = -x^2 + 4x + 2$
   $y = 2 - x$

EXAMPLE 4   ☑ **Try It!** **Solve Systems Using Substitution**

4. Could you have used elimination or graphing to solve this linear-quadratic system of equations? Explain.

HABITS OF MIND

Construct Arguments Explain when a solution to a linear-quadratic system of equations is not included as part of the solution to a problem. Ⓒ **MP.3**

✓ Do You UNDERSTAND?

1. ❓ **ESSENTIAL QUESTION** How is solving linear-quadratic systems of equations similar to and different from solving systems of linear equations?

2. Error Analysis A student claims that a linear-quadratic system of equations has three solutions. Explain the error the student made. ⓒ **MP.3**

3. Vocabulary What are the characteristics of a *linear-quadratic system* of equations?

4. Reason What system of equations could you use to solve the equation $x^2 - 3 = 7$? Explain. ⓒ **MP.2**

Do You KNOW HOW?

Rewrite each equation as a system of equations.

5. $3 = x^2 + 2x$

6. $x = x^2 - 5$

7. $2x^2 - 5 = x + 7$

8. $x^2 - 2x + 3 = x + 4$

Find the solution of each system of equations.

9. $\begin{cases} y = x^2 + 3x + 1 \\ y = -x + 1 \end{cases}$

10. $\begin{cases} y = x^2 + 1 \\ y = -2x \end{cases}$

11.

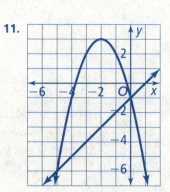

EXPLORE & REASON

One of the strangest mysteries in archaeology was discovered in the Diquís Delta of Costa Rica. Hundreds of sphere-shaped stones were found.

A great circle is the circle with the greatest diameter that can be drawn on any given sphere.

A. The formula for the surface area of a sphere is $SA = 4\pi r^2$. What is the surface area of the stone in terms of the circumference of the great circle?

B. The circumferences of the great circles of spheres range in size from about 6 cm to 6 m. Make a graph that represents circumference as a function of surface area.

C. Look for Relationships What similarities and differences do you notice about the graph from Part B and the graph of a quadratic function? © **MP.7**

HABITS OF MIND

Look for Relationships What are the domain and range of the circumference function? How do they compare to the domain and range of a quadratic function? © **MP.7**

EXAMPLE 1 ☑ Try It! Key Features of Square Root Functions

1. Graph each function. What are the intercepts, domain, and range of the function?

a. $p(x) = -\sqrt{x}$

b. $q(x) = \sqrt{\dfrac{x}{10}}$

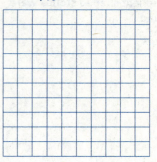

EXAMPLE 2 ☑ Try It! Translations of Square Root Functions

2. How does each graph compare to the graph of $f(x) = \sqrt{x}$?

a. $g(x) = \sqrt{x} - 4$

b. $p(x) = \sqrt{x - 10}$

HABITS OF MIND

Communicate Precisely Name the different types of transformations that can be made to the graph of $f(x) = \sqrt{x}$ and how they affect the graph. ⓒ **MP.6**

EXAMPLE 3   ✅ **Try It! Rate of Change of a Square Root Function**

3. For the function $h(x) = \sqrt{2x}$, find $h(8)$, $h(10)$, and $h(12)$. Then find the average rate of change of the function over each interval.

a. $8 \leq x \leq 10$

b. $10 \leq x \leq 12$

EXAMPLE 4   ✅ **Try It! Compare Square Root Functions**

4. To the nearest thousandth, evaluate each function for the given value of the variable.

a. $v(x) = \frac{\sqrt{x}}{10}$; $x = 17$

b. $w(x) = \sqrt{\frac{x}{10}}$; $x = 17$

HABITS OF MIND

Reason Why does the given interval affect the rate of change of a square root function? ⓒ **MP.2**

Do You UNDERSTAND?

1.  **ESSENTIAL QUESTION** What key features are shared among the square root function and translations of the square function?

2. **Use Structure** Explain why each function is, or is not, a a translation of the square root function. © **MP.7**

   a. $h(x) = 2\sqrt{x+1}$

   b. $g(x) = \sqrt{x+2} - 3$

3. **Error Analysis** A student identified (6, 12) and (9, 27) as points on the graph of the function $f(x) = \sqrt{3x}$. What error did the student make? © **MP.3**

4. **Reason** What is the domain of $f(x) = \sqrt{x+3}$? © **MP.2**

Do You KNOW HOW?

How does each graph compare to the graph of $f(x) = \sqrt{x}$?

5. $g(x) = \sqrt{x} - 2$ 6. $h(x) = \sqrt{x} - 5$

7. $p(x) = 5 + \sqrt{x}$ 8. $q(x) = \sqrt{7+x}$

For the given function, find the average rate of change to the nearest hundredth over the given interval.

9. $f(x) = \sqrt{x+7}$; $2 \leq x \leq 10$

10. $g(x) = \sqrt{x+7}$; $-3 \leq x \leq 5$

11. $h(x) = \sqrt{2x}$; $0 \leq x \leq 10$

CRITIQUE & EXPLAIN

Emilia wrote several radical expressions on the whiteboard.

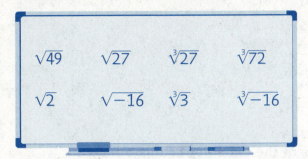

$\sqrt{49}$ $\sqrt{27}$ $\sqrt[3]{27}$ $\sqrt[3]{72}$

$\sqrt{2}$ $\sqrt{-16}$ $\sqrt[3]{3}$ $\sqrt[3]{-16}$

A. Evaluate each expression, and explain how to plot each value on a real number line.

B. Explain how evaluating a cube root function is different from evaluating a square root function.

C. Construct Arguments Emilia states that it is not possible to plot either $\sqrt{-16}$ or $\sqrt[3]{-16}$ on the real number line. Do you agree? Explain. © **MP.3**

HABITS OF MIND

Make Sense and Persevere Write the following numbers in the order they would appear from left to right on a real number line: $\sqrt{8}$, $\sqrt[3]{8}$, $\sqrt[3]{-8}$, $\sqrt{16}$. © **MP.1**

✅ Assess

EXAMPLE 1 ☑ **Try It!** **Key Features of Cube Root Functions**

1. What are the maximum and minimum values for $f(x) = \sqrt[3]{x}$ over the interval $-27 \leq x \leq 27$?

EXAMPLE 2 ☑ **Try It!** **Translations of the Cube Root Function**

2. Compare the graph of each function to the graph of $f(x) = \sqrt[3]{x}$.

a. $g(x) = \sqrt[3]{x} - 2$

b. $p(x) = \sqrt[3]{x + 1}$

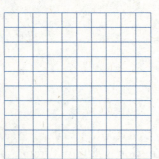
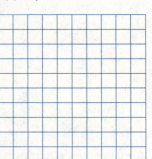

EXAMPLE 3 ☑ **Try It!** **Interpret the Attributes of a Cube Root Function**

3. A cube has a volume of 10 cm³. A larger cube has a volume of x cm³. Consider the function $f(x) = \sqrt[3]{x - 10}$. What do the values $f(3)$ and $f(4)$ represent?

HABITS OF MIND

Communicate Precisely How is transforming cube root functions similar to transforming square root functions? How is it different? Ⓒ **MP.6**

EXAMPLE 4 ☑ **Try It!** **Compare Rates of Change of a Function**

4. Compare the average rates of change for $f(x) = 2\sqrt[3]{x - 3}$ over the intervals $-12 \leq x \leq -8$ and $-4 \leq x \leq 0$.

EXAMPLE 5 ☑ **Try It!** **Compare Rates of Change of Two Functions**

5. Which function has the greater average rate of change over the interval $-5 \leq x \leq 0$: the translation of $f(x) = \sqrt[3]{x}$ to the right 1 unit and up 2 units, or the function $r(x) = \sqrt[3]{x} + 3$?

HABITS OF MIND

Use Appropriate Tools Which method of comparing functions do you prefer? Justify your answer. Ⓒ **MP.5**

☑ Do You UNDERSTAND?

1. ESSENTIAL QUESTION What are the key features of the cube root function?

2. Error Analysis Timothy uses his calculator to investigate the domain and range of $f(x) = \sqrt[3]{x}$. He estimates the range as $-2 \le y \le 2$. What is the error that Timothy made? © **MP.3**

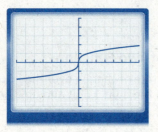

3. Look for Relationships Explain how the graph of $f(x) = \sqrt[3]{x}$ is related to the graph of $g(x) = -\sqrt[3]{x}$. © **MP.7**

Do You KNOW HOW?

4. Identify the domain and range of $s(x) = \sqrt[3]{3x}$.

5. Describe how the graph of $g(x) = \sqrt[3]{x} - 3$ is related to the graph of $f(x) = \sqrt[3]{x}$.

6. Find the maximum and minimum values of $f(x) = \sqrt[3]{x - 1}$ for $-2 \le x \le 9$.

7. Calculate the average rate of change of $g(x) = \sqrt[3]{x} + 3$ for $4 \le x \le 7$.

8. Describe how the graph of $g(x) = \sqrt[3]{x - 4}$ is related to the graph of $f(x) = \sqrt{x}$.

MODEL & DISCUSS

Each table represents part of a function.

x	f(x)
−2	1
−1	4
0	5
1	4
2	1

x	g(x)
−2	20
−1	10
0	5
1	2.5
2	1.25

x	h(x)
−2	11
−1	8
0	5
1	2
2	−1

x	j(x)
−2	2
−1	1
0	0
1	1
2	2

x	k(x)
−2	21
−1	11
0	5
1	3
2	5

 SavvasRealize.com

A. Plot the points of each function on a graph. Describe what you know about each function.

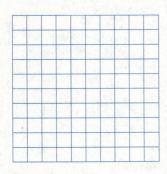
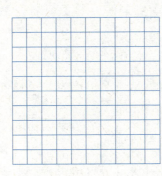
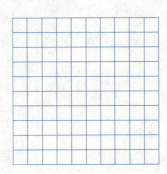

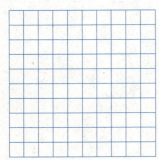
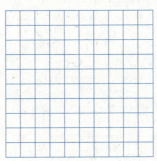

B. Look for Relationships Which functions are related? Explain your reasoning. MP.7

HABITS OF MIND

Use Structure Based on the given points, guess a reasonable domain and range for each function. Ⓒ MP.7

EXAMPLE 1 ☑ **Try It!** **Analyze Domain and Range**

1. Explain how you can determine the ranges of *h* and *j* from the expressions that define them.

EXAMPLE 2 ☑ **Try It!** **Analyze Maximum and Minimum Values**

2. Does each function have a maximum value and/or a minimum value? Sketch the graph of each function to help you.

a. $f(x) = x^2 - 3x + 1$

b. $g(x) = 2\sqrt{x} + 1$

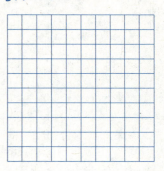

c. $h(x) = \sqrt[3]{8(x - 1)} + 5$

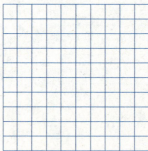

HABITS OF MIND

Look for Relationships What do the graphs of the the functions in parts *b* and *c* have in common? © **MP.7**

EXAMPLE 3   ☑ **Try It!** Understand Axes of Symmetry

3. Does each type of function have an axis of symmetry? Sketch graphs to help you.

   a. $g(x) = 2^x$ b. $h(x) = \sqrt[3]{x} + 4$

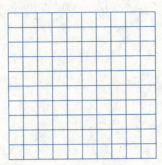   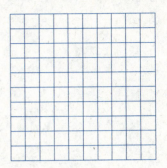

EXAMPLE 4   ☑ **Try It!** Analyze End Behaviors of Graphs

4. Compare the end behaviors of the functions.

   $f(x) = 2^{x+2}$ $g(x) = \left(\frac{1}{3}\right)^x + 4$ $h(x) = -x^2 + 2x + 1$

HABITS OF MIND

Reason Which types of transformations affect the end behavior of a function? Explain. © MP.2

☑ Do You UNDERSTAND?

1. ❓ ESSENTIAL QUESTION ▷ What can you learn about a function by analyzing its graph?

2. Error Analysis Kona states that the maximum value of $f(x) = -2^x$ is 0. Explain Kona's error. Ⓒ MP.3

3. Look for Relationships How are behaviors of quadratic functions like those of the absolute value function? Ⓒ MP.7

Do You KNOW HOW?

For each function identify the domain and range, state the maximum and minimum values, identify the axis of symmetry, if it exists, and describe the end behavior.

4. $f(x) = \sqrt{x - 5}$

5. $g(x) = x^2 + 2x + 1$

6. $h(x) = 2 - |x + 6|$

Go Online | SavvasRealize.com

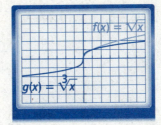

CRITIQUE & EXPLAIN

The figure shows $f(x) = \sqrt{x}$ and $g(x) = \sqrt[3]{x}$. Venetta says that vertical translations will work in the same way for these functions as they do for quadratic and exponential functions. Tonya disagrees.

A. For $f(x) + c$ and $g(x) + c$, what translation do you expect when c is positive? When c is negative?

B. **Generalize** Which student is correct? Explain your answer. © MP.8

HABITS OF MIND

Reason Do you think that horizontal translations will work in the same way for square root and cube root functions as they do for quadratic and exponential functions? Justify your answer. © MP.2

 ☑ Assess

EXAMPLE 1 ☑ **Try It!** **Vertical Translations**

1. For each function $g(x) = f(x) + k$, how does the value of k affect the graph of function f?

   a. $g(x) = f(x) + 7$

   b. $g(x) = f(x) - 9$

EXAMPLE 2 ☑ **Try It!** **Analyze Horizontal Translations**

2. For each function $g(x) = f(x - h)$, how does the value of h affect the graph of function f?

   a. $g(x) = f(x - 8)$

   b. $g(x) = f(x + 7)$

HABITS OF MIND

Communicate Precisely Why is it not necessary to know the function represented by f in Try It! problems 1 and 2? ⓒ **MP.6**

EXAMPLE 3 ☑ **Try It! Combine Translations**

3. Graph f and $g(x) = f(x - 2) + 3$.

   a. $f(x) = x^2$

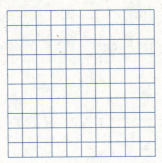

   b. $f(x) = 2^x$

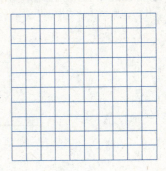

   c. $f(x) = \sqrt{x}$

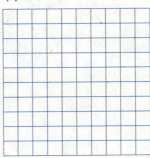

- -

HABITS OF MIND

Look for Relationships How do the domains and ranges of f and g compare when f is a quadratic, exponential, or a square root function? ⓒ **MP.7**

Do You UNDERSTAND?

1. ? **ESSENTIAL QUESTION** Do horizontal and vertical translations work in the same way for all types of functions?

2. Use Structure How can translations help you sketch the graph of $f(x) = x^2 + 8x + 16$? © MP.7

3. Error Analysis Ashton says that $f(x) = \sqrt{x - 3}$ has domain $x \geq -3$. Is Ashton correct? Explain your reasoning. © MP.3

4. Construct Arguments Explain why adding a number to the output of a function shifts its graph vertically. © MP.3

Do You KNOW HOW?

Sketch the graph of each function.

5. $f(x) = |x| + 4$

6. $f(x) = (x - 2)^3$

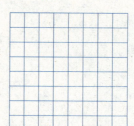 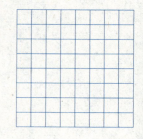

7. $f(x) = \sqrt{x + 2}$

8. $f(x) = 3^x - 5$

9. $f(x) = (x - 1)^2 - 2$

10. $f(x) = \sqrt{x + 4} + 3$

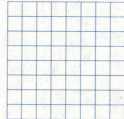 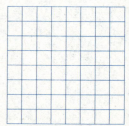

11. What is the equation of the graph?

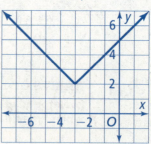

EXPLORE & REASON

The graphs of three quadratic functions g, h, and j all have a vertex of (0, 0). Additional points that lie on the graph of each function are shown.

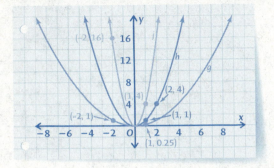

A. Write a quadratic function for each parabola.

B. Communicate Precisely How are these expressions similar? How are they different? © MP.6

C. Using your knowledge of compressions and stretches of other functions and your answers to parts A and B, describe how to write a vertical stretch or compression of $f(x) = \sqrt{x}$ to.

HABITS OF MIND

Reason Can you determine if the graph of $g(x) = ax^2$ is a vertical stretch or compression of the graph $f(x) = x^2$ or a horizontal stretch or compression of the graph f? Explain. © MP.2

EXAMPLE 1 ✅ **Try It!** **Analyze Reflections Across the *x*-Axis**

1. Write a function with a graph that is the reflection of the graph of *f* across the *x*-axis.

   a. $f(x) = x$

   b. $f(x) = \sqrt{x}$

EXAMPLE 2 ✅ **Try It!** **Analyze Vertical Stretches of Graphs**

2. Write a function with a graph that is a vertical stretch of the graph of *f*, away from the *x*-axis.

   a. $f(x) = x$

   b. $f(x) = \sqrt{x}$

EXAMPLE 3 ✅ **Try It!** **Analyze Vertical Compressions of Graphs**

3. Write a function with a graph that is a vertical compression of the graph of *f*, toward the *x*-axis.

   a. $f(x) = \sqrt{x}$

   b. $f(x) = |x|$

HABITS OF MIND

Make Sense and Persevere Will the transformed function be wider or narrower than its parent function? Ⓒ **MP.1**

   a. $f(x) = x^6$
   $g(x) = 0.1x^6$

   b. $f(x) = \sqrt[3]{x^5}$
   $g(x) = \frac{12}{5}\sqrt[3]{x^5}$

EXAMPLE 4 ☑ **Try It!** **Analyze Horizontal Stretches of Graphs**

4. Why is $g(x) = 0.2x + 2$ a horizontal stretch of $f(x) = x + 2$?

EXAMPLE 5 ☑ **Try It!** **Analyze Horizontal Compressions of Graphs**

5. Write a function with a graph that is a horizontal compression of the graph of f, toward the y-axis.

a. $f(x) = \sqrt[3]{x}$

b. $f(x) = x^2$

HABITS OF MIND

Communicate Precisely Explain the different algebraic processes for vertically stretching or compressing a graph and for horizontally stretching or compressing a graph. Ⓒ **MP.6**

Do You UNDERSTAND?

1. **ESSENTIAL QUESTION** What change to a function will result in a vertical or horizontal stretch or compression of its graph?

2. **Error Analysis** A student says that the graph of the function $g(x) = 0.4f(x)$ is a horizontal compression of the function f. Explain the error the student made. © MP.3

3. **Communicate Precisely** Compare and contrast a vertical stretch and a horizontal stretch. © MP.6

4. **Reason** Given the function f and the constant k, write the general form for a horizontal stretch of the function. Make sure to include any constraints on k. © MP.2

Do You KNOW HOW?

Tell whether the graph of g is a reflection across the x-axis of the graph of f.

5. $f(x) = 4x + 5$
   $g(x) = -4x - 5$

6. $f(x) = -3x^2 + 7$
   $g(x) = 3x^2 + 7$

Given $k = 8$, describe how the graph of each function relates to f.

7. $g(x) = f(kx)$

8. $g(x) = kf(x)$

9. Identify whether a horizontal stretch or compression was used to produce the graph of g given the graph of f shown below.

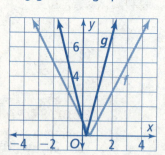

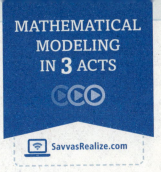
▶ Edgy Tiles

For more than 3,000 years, people have glazed ceramics and other materials to make decorative tile patterns. Tiles used to be used only in important buildings or by the very rich, but now you can find tiles in almost any house.

Before you start tiling a wall, floor, or other surface, it's important to plan out how your design will look. Think about this during the Mathematical Modeling in 3 Acts lesson.

ACT 1

1. What is the first question that comes to mind after watching the video?

2. Write down the Main Question you will answer.

3. Make an initial conjecture that answers this Main Question.

4. Explain how you arrived at your conjecture.

5. What information will be useful to know to answer the main question? How can you get it? How will you use that information?

ACT 2

6. Use the math that you have learned in the topic to refine your conjecture.

ACT 3

7. Did your refined conjecture match the actual answer exactly? If not, what might explain the difference?

EXPLORE & REASON

The graphs of $f(x) = x^2$ and $g(x) = x^2 + 3$ are shown.

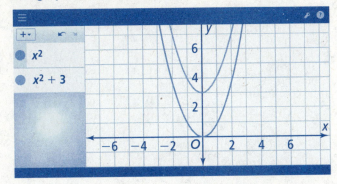

A. Compare the domain and range of each function.

B. Graph another function of the form $f(x) = x^2 + c$ using a different constant added to x^2.

C. **Look for Relationships** Does changing a function by adding a constant alter the domain of the function? Does changing a function by adding a constant alter the range of the function? Explain. © **MP.7**

HABITS OF MIND

Use Structure What other key features of the graph change by adding a constant? © **MP.7**

EXAMPLE 1 ☑ **Try It!** Add and Subtract Functions

1. If $f(x) = 15x^2 - 8x + 4$ and $g(x) = 11x + 6$, what is $f - g$?

EXAMPLE 2 ☑ **Try It!** Multiply Functions

2. Find the product of f and g. What are the domain and the range of the product?

a. $f(x) = \sqrt{x}$
   $g(x) = 2x - 1$

b. $f(x) = 3x^2 + 4$
   $g(x) = 2^x$

HABITS OF MIND

Construct Arguments A student claims that for any two functions, the domain and range of the product of the functions will be the same as the domain and range of the sum of the functions. Is the student correct? Explain. Provide a counterexample if the student is incorrect. Ⓒ **MP.3**

EXAMPLE 3   ☑ **Try It!** **Apply Function Operations**

3. Suppose the cylinder in Example 3 is not sealed, so the total surface area includes only the area of the bottom and the lateral surface area. What dimensions would yield a total surface area of about 120 ft²?

HABITS OF MIND

Make Sense and Persevere Compare the domains and ranges of f, g, and $f + g$. Explain why your answer makes sense for this context. © **MP.1**

Do You UNDERSTAND?

1. **? ESSENTIAL QUESTION** How can you extend addition, subtraction, and multiplication from numbers to functions?

2. **Use Structure** What property is useful when subtracting a function that has multiple terms? © **MP.7**

3. **Use Appropriate Tools** Describe how you can use a graph to find the domain and range of two combined functions. © **MP.5**

4. **Error Analysis** A student claimed that the functions $f(x) = \sqrt{x}$ and $g(x) = 2x - 5$ cannot be combined because there are no like terms. Explain the error the student made. © **MP.3**

Do You KNOW HOW?

Find $f + g$.

5. $f(x) = 4x + 1$
$g(x) = 2x^2 - 5x$

6. $f(x) = x^2$
$g(x) = 3^x$

Find $f - g$.

7. $f(x) = 4x^2$
$g(x) = x^2 + 2x + 7$

8. $f(x) = 6x + 5$
$g(x) = \sqrt{2x}$

Find $f \cdot g$.

9. $f(x) = 3x^2 - 2$
$g(x) = x^2 - 4x$

10. $f(x) = 6x$
$g(x) = 8^x$

EXPLORE & REASON

The tables of data show food orders for different parties.

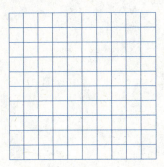

Pizzeria A

Pizzas ordered (x)	Sandwiches ordered (y)
2	10
4	7
6	5
8	2

Pizzeria B

Sandwiches ordered (x)	Pizzas ordered (y)
2	8
5	6
7	4
10	2

A. Graph the data points shown in the tables. Use a different color for each data set.

B. Look for Relationships What observations can you make about the graphs of the data in the two tables? © **MP.7**

C. What similarities and differences do you notice about the data?

HABITS OF MIND

Make Sense and Persevere Find a function to model each of the sets of data points. © **MP.1**

Assess

EXAMPLE 1 ☑ **Try It!** Understand Inverse Functions

1. How is the slope of f^{-1} related to the slope of f?

EXAMPLE 2 ☑ **Try It!** Graph Inverse Functions

2. Graph each function and its inverse.

a. $f(x) = 3x - 2$

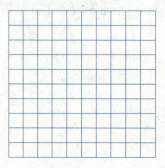

b. $f(x) = 2x^2, x \geq 0$

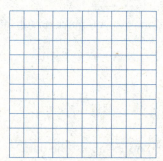

HABITS OF MIND

Communicate Precisely Explain why the inverse of a function can be described as the reflection of the function across the line $y = x$. Ⓒ **MP.6**

EXAMPLE 3   ☑ **Try It!** **Find the Inverse of a Function Algebraically**

3. Find the inverse of each function.

   a. $f(x) = 3x^2, x \geq 0$

   b. $f(x) = x - 7$

EXAMPLE 4   ☑ **Try It!** **Interpret Inverse Functions**

4. Suppose the credit card company changes the program so Keenan earns 1 mile for every $8 he spends. How would that change the amount of money Keenan needs to spend to earn the miles for his trip?

HABITS OF MIND

Use Appropriate Tools Explain how you could use graphing to solve the previous problem. © **MP.5**

Do You UNDERSTAND?

1. **ESSENTIAL QUESTION** How can you use inverse functions to help solve problems?

2. **Error Analysis** A student claims that the graph of the inverse of a function is a reflection across the *x*-axis of the graph of the original function. Explain the error the student made. ©️ **MP.3**

3. **Vocabulary** Does every function have an inverse function? Explain.

4. **Reason** If the graph of a function crosses the *x*-axis twice, does the function have an inverse function? Explain. ©️ **MP.2**

Do You KNOW HOW?

Copy and complete each table of values for the function. Then make a table of values for the inverse of the function.

5. $y = -2x + 3$

x	y
0	■
1	■
2	■
3	■

6. $y = 8x$

x	y
0	■
1	■
2	■
3	■

Write the inverse of each function.

7. $f(x) = 2x + 11$

8. $f(x) = \sqrt{x}$

MODEL & DISCUSS

MARKET RESEARCHERS WANTED!

A clothing company is designing a new line of shirts. Look around your classroom and collect data about the color of top worn by each student. If a student's top has multiple colors, choose the most prevalent one.

A. Explain why you chose to organize the data the way that you did.

B. How do you think the company could use these data?

C. Use Appropriate Tools How would you display these data in a presentation? © MP.5

HABITS OF MIND

Reason What other information could you collect about the different types of shirts in your classroom? How could you organize these data? © MP.2

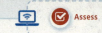
EXAMPLE 1 ☑ **Try It!** **Represent and Interpret Data in a Dot Plot**

1. What might account for the outlier?

EXAMPLE 2 ☑ **Try It!** **Represent and Interpret Data in a Histogram**

2. What age group would be a good match for products advertised on this TV show? Explain.

HABITS OF MIND

Look for Relationships How is interpreting a histogram similar to interpreting a dot plot? How is it different? Ⓒ **MP.7**

EXAMPLE 3 ☑ **Try It! Represent and Interpret Data in a Box Plot**

3. Suppose Kaitlyn wants to make the statement that 25% of the students raised over a certain amount. What is that amount? Explain.

EXAMPLE 4 ☑ **Try It! Choose a Data Display**

4. Which data display should Helena use if she wants to know what percent of the teams scored higher than her team? Explain.

HABITS OF MIND

Use Appropriate Tools When is it useful to display data as a dot plot? When is it useful to display data as a histogram? When is it useful to display data as a box plot? ⓒ **MP.5**

Do You UNDERSTAND?

1. **ESSENTIAL QUESTION** What information about data sets can you get from different data displays?

2. **Communicate Precisely** How is a dot plot different from a box plot? How are they similar? © MP.6

3. **Use Appropriate Tools** If you want to see data values grouped in intervals, which data display should you choose? Explain. © MP.5

4. **Error Analysis** Taylor says you can determine the mean of a data set from its box plot. Is Taylor correct? Explain your reasoning. © MP.3

5. **Use Structure** Can you determine the minimum and maximum values of a data set simply by looking at its dot plot? Histogram? Box plot? Explain. © MP.7

Do You KNOW HOW?

Use the data set shown for exercises 6–11.

7	5	8	15	4
9	10	1	12	8
13	7	11	8	10

6. Make a dot plot for the data. What information does the display reveal about the data set?

7. Make a histogram for the data. What information does the display reveal about the data set?

8. Make a box plot for the data. What information does the display reveal about the data set?

Identify the most appropriate data display to answer each question about the data set. Justify your response.

9. What is the median of the data set?

10. How many data values are greater than 7?

11. How many values fall in the interval 10 to 12?

CRITIQUE & EXPLAIN

The prices of paintings sold at two galleries in the last month are shown. Stacy and Diego both have a painting they want to sell.

- Stacy wants Gallery I to sell her painting because it has the highest sales price.
- Diego wants Gallery II to sell his painting because it has the most consistent sales prices.

Gallery I
$500 $800 $1,200
$750 $550 $15,000

Gallery II
$2,800 $3,500 $3,000
$2,750 $3,100

A. Do you agree with Stacy or Diego? Explain your reasoning.

B. **Reasoning** What reason(s) could there be for the differences in sales prices between the two galleries and for the outlier in Gallery I? © **MP.2**

HABITS OF MIND

Make Sense and Persevere What is the mean sales price for the paintings at Gallery I? What is the mean sales price for the paintings at Gallery II? © **MP.1**

EXAMPLE 1 ☑ **Try It!** Compare Data Sets Displayed in Dot Plots

1. How does the outlier in the second data set affect the mean and the MAD?

EXAMPLE 2 ☑ **Try It!** Compare Data Sets Displayed in Box Plots

2. How does the IQR compare to the range for each school?

HABITS OF MIND

Use Appropriate Tools Does the information given by a box plot allow you to determine the mean of a set of data? © **MP.5**

EXAMPLE 3   ☑ **Try It!** **Compare Data Sets Displayed in Histograms**

3. If the marketing team wants to advertise a product that is targeted at adults 25–34, during which show should they advertise? Explain.

EXAMPLE 4   ☑ **Try It!** **Make Observations With Data Displays**

4. a. Provide a possible explanation for each of the observations that was made.

    b. Make 2 more observations about the data that Nadia collected.

HABITS OF MIND

Use Appropriate Tools Does the type of graph you create with given data change the observations that can be made from the data display? Explain. © **MP.6**

Do You UNDERSTAND?

1. **ESSENTIAL QUESTION** How can you use measures of center and spread to compare data sets?

2. Communicate Precisely How are the MAD and the IQR similar? How are they different? Ⓒ **MP.6**

3. Reason When comparing two sets of data, it is common to look at the means. Why might the MAD be a useful piece of information to compare in addition to the mean? Ⓒ **MP.2**

4. Error Analysis Val says that if the minimum and maximum values of two data sets are the same, the median will be the same. Is Val correct? Explain. Ⓒ **MP.3**

Do You KNOW HOW?

Use the two data sets.

Data Set A				
86	87	98	85	90
94	89	83	76	84
83	90	87	87	86

Data Set B				
80	89	70	75	87
88	75	87	89	81
84	87	88	81	87

5. How do the means compare?

6. How do the MADs compare?

7. How do the medians compare?

8. How do the IQRs compare?

9. Which measures of center and spread are better for comparing data sets A and B? Explain.

EXPLORE & REASON

A meteorologist looks at measures of center to summarize the last 10 days of actual high temperatures.

SUN	MON	TUE	WED	THU	FRI	SAT	SUN	MON	TUE
75°	73°	72°	75°	73°	75°	76°	90°	95°	95°

Average High 80°

A. Find the median, mean, and mode of the data.

B. Which of the three measures of center seems to be the most accurate in describing the data? Explain.

C. Communicate Precisely How can you describe the data? © MP.6

HABITS OF MIND

Reason Explain how the central tendencies of the data would shift if the temperatures 90°, 95°, and 95° were not included. © MP.2

EXAMPLE 1 **Try It!** Interpret the Shape of a Distribution

1. Suppose a third category of dogs has a mean of 40 lb and a median of 32 lb. What can you infer about the shape of the histogram for the dogs in this category?

EXAMPLE 2 **Try It!** Interpret the Shape of a Skewed Data Display

2. How do skewed data affect the mean in this context?

HABITS OF MIND

Construct Arguments A student reasons that because most of the data in a histogram lie on the right side of the graph, the data must be skewed right. Is this student correct? Justify your answer. © **MP.3**

EXAMPLE 3   ☑ **Try It!** **Compare Shapes of Skewed Data Displays**

3. What does the shape of the histogram for the second sample tell you about the data?

EXAMPLE 4   ☑ **Try It!** **Interpret the Shape of a Symmetric Data Display**

4. Suppose the quality control manager adds another 10 bagels to the third sample. If 5 of the bagels are 78 g each, and 5 of the bagels are 106 g each, would that affect the mean and median weights? Explain.

EXAMPLE 5   ☑ **Try It!** **Comparing the Shapes of Data Sets**

5. Suppose a fourth school district offers Jennifer a job. School District 401 has a mean salary of $57,000 and a median salary of $49,000. Should Jennifer consider accepting the job offer with School District 401? Explain.

HABITS OF MIND

Reason If the mean and median of a set of data are equal, or nearly equal, are the data necessarily symmetric? Explain. ⓒ **MP.2**

Do You UNDERSTAND?

1. 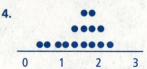 **ESSENTIAL QUESTION** How does the shape of a data set help you understand the data?

2. **Use Structure** How are the shapes of dot plots, histograms, and box plots similar? How are they different? © **MP.7**

3. **Error Analysis** Nicholas says that the display for a skewed data distribution is symmetrical about the mean. Is Nicholas correct? Explain your reasoning. © **MP.3**

Do You KNOW HOW?

Tell whether each display is skewed left, skewed right, or symmetric. Interpret what the display tells you about the data set.

4.

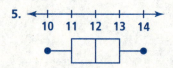

5.

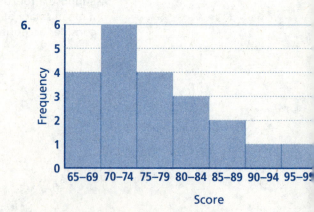

6.

MODEL & DISCUSS

A meteorologist compares the high temperatures for two cities during the past 10 days.

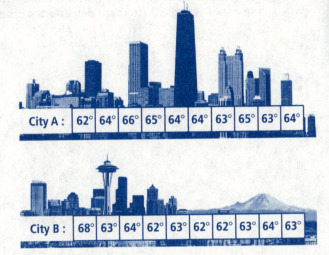

City A : 62° 64° 66° 65° 64° 64° 63° 65° 63° 64°

City B : 68° 63° 64° 62° 63° 62° 62° 63° 64° 63°

A. Create a data display for each city's high temperatures.

B. Use Structure What does the shape of each data display indicate about the data set and the measures of center? **© MP.7**

HABITS OF MIND

Make Sense and Persevere What is the range of each data set? What is the mean of each data set? **© MP.1**

 Assess

EXAMPLE 1 ☑ **Try It!** **Interpret the Variability of a Data Set**

1. What is the lifespan of light bulbs that are within 2 standard deviations of the mean? Within 3 standard deviations of the mean?

HABITS OF MIND

Reason Does any of the data from Example 1 fall three standard deviations above or below the mean? In general, is it possible for data to fall more than two standard deviations above or below the mean? Explain. © **MP.2**

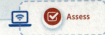

EXAMPLE 2 ☑ **Try It!** **Calculate the Standard Deviation of a Sample**

2. The table shows the number of cars sold by the auto sales associate over the next eight-week period. How much variability do the data show?

12	14	29	10	17	16	18	16

EXAMPLE 3 ☑ **Try It!** **Find Standard Deviation of a Population**

3. What was the range of points that the team scored in 95% of their regular season games?

EXAMPLE 4 ☑ **Try It!** **Compare Data Sets Using Standard Deviation**

4. Compare Brand C, with mean 1,250 hours and standard deviation 83 hours, to Brands A and B.

HABITS OF MIND

Communicate Precisely What does a large standard deviation indicate? © **MP.6**

Do You UNDERSTAND?

1. **? ESSENTIAL QUESTION** Why does the way in which data are spread out matter?

2. **Generalize** What are the steps in finding standard deviation? Ⓒ **MP.8**

3. **Error Analysis** Marisol says that standard deviation is a measure of how much the values in a data set deviate from the median. Is Marisol correct? Explain. Ⓒ **MP.3**

4. **Use Structure** If you add 10 to every data value in a set, what happens to the mean, range, and standard deviation. Why? Ⓒ **MP.7**

Do You KNOW HOW?

Sample A: 1, 2, 2, 5, 5, 5, 6, 6

Sample B: 5, 9, 9, 10, 10, 10, 11, 11

5. What can you determine by using range to compare the spread of the two data sets?

6. Find the standard deviation for each data set.

7. How can you use standard deviation to compare the spread of each data set?

8. Based on the histogram, what data values are within one standard deviation of the mean?

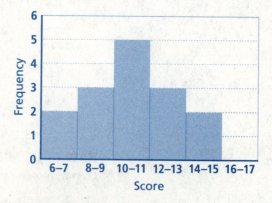

Mean: 11.05
Standard Deviation: 2.40

EXPLORE & REASON

Baseball teams at a high school and a college play at the same stadium. Results for every game last season are given for both teams. There were no ties.

⋆ ☆☆ *Wins!* ☆⋆⋆	HOME	AWAY
WEST MOUNTAIN HIGH SCHOOL	11 OUT OF 16	08 OUT OF 14
BIG MOUNTAIN COLLEGE	18 OUT OF 26	18 OUT OF 30

A. How could you organize the data in table form?

B. **Look for Relationships** How would you analyze the data to determine whether the data support the claim that the team that plays at home is more likely to win? © **MP.7**

HABITS OF MIND

Make Sense and Persevere What percentage of the West Mountain High School team's total games are home wins? What percentage of the Big Mountain College team's total games are away losses? © **MP.1**

☑ Assess

EXAMPLE 1 ☑ **Try It!** **Interpret a Two-Way Frequency Table**

    1. What do the marginal frequencies tell you about the number of male and female respondents?

EXAMPLE 2 ☑ **Try It!** **Interpret a Two-Way Relative Frequency Table**

    2. How can you tell whether a greater percent of customers surveyed selected veggie burger or veggie pizza?

HABITS OF MIND

Communicate Precisely How does joint relative frequency relate to joint frequency? How does marginal relative frequency relate to marginal frequency? ⓒ **MP.6**

📶 Go Online | SavvasRealize.com

EXAMPLE 3 ☑ **Try It!** **Calculate Conditional Relative Frequency**

3. What conclusion could the marketing team make about male and female preferences for veggie pizza? Justify your answer.

EXAMPLE 4 ☑ **Try It!** **Interpret Conditional Relative Frequency**

4. What conclusion could you draw if the percentages for male and female customers were the same across the rows in this table?

EXAMPLE 5 ☑ **Try It!** **Interpret Data Frequencies**

5. What does the conditional relative frequency $\frac{72}{137}$ represent in this context?

HABITS OF MIND

Look for Relationships Why can there be multiple values for the conditional relative frequency? Ⓒ MP.7

Assess

Do You UNDERSTAND?

1. **ESSENTIAL QUESTION** How can you use two-way frequency tables to analyze data?

2. **Communicate Precisely** How are joint frequencies and marginal frequencies similar? How are they different? **© MP.6**

3. **Look for Relationships** How are conditional relative frequencies related to joint frequencies and marginal frequencies? **© MP.7**

4. **Error Analysis** Zhang says that the marginal relative frequency for a given variable is 10. Could Zhang be correct? Explain your reasoning. **© MP.3**

Do You KNOW HOW?

In a survey, customers select Item A or Item B. Item A is selected by 20 males and 10 females. Of 20 customers who select Item B, five are males.

5. Make a two-way frequency table to organize the data.

6. Make a two-way relative frequency table to organize the data.

7. Calculate conditional relative frequencies for males and females. Is it reasonable to conclude that males prefer Item A more than females do?

8. Calculate conditional relative frequencies for Item A and Item B. Is it reasonable to conclude that a customer who prefers Item B is more likely to be a female than a male?

Text Message

Text messages used be just that: text only. Now you can send multimedia messages (or MMS) with emojis, images, audio, and videos. Did you know Finland was the first country to offer text messaging to phone customers?

Some people send and receive so many texts that they use textspeak to make typing faster. RU 1 of them? You will see one person keep track of his text messages in this Modeling Mathematics in 3 Acts lesson.

SavvasRealize.com

ACT 1 **Identify the Problem**

1. What is the first question that comes to mind after watching the video?

2. Write down the Main Question you will answer about what you saw in the video.

3. Make an initial conjecture that answers this main question.

4. Explain how you arrived at your conjecture.

5. What information will be useful to know to answer the main question? How can you get it? How will you use that information?

ACT 2 › Develop a Model

6. Use the math that you have learned in this Topic to refine your conjecture.

ACT 3 › Interpret the Results

7. Is your refined conjecture between the highs and lows you set up earlier?

8. Did your refined conjecture match the actual answer exactly? If not, what might explain the difference?